1st Nephi: *a brief theological introduction*

This publication was made possible by generous support from the Laura F. Willes Center for Book of Mormon Studies, part of the Neal A. Maxwell Institute for Religious Scholarship at Brigham Young University.

Published by the Neal A. Maxwell Institute for Religious Scholarship, Brigham Young University, Provo, Utah. The copyright for the 2013 text of The Book of Mormon is held by The Church of Jesus Christ of Latter-day Saints, Salt Lake City, Utah; that text is quoted throughout, and used by permission.

Printed in the United States of America

ISBN: 978-0-8425-0007-4

LIBRARY OF CONGRESS CONTROL NUMBER: 2019954814

1st Nephi

a brief theological introduction

BRIGHAM YOUNG UNIVERSITY

NEAL A. MAXWELL INSTITUTE

PROVO, UTAH

Joseph M. Spencer

The Book of Mormon: brief theological introductions series seeks Christ in scripture by combining intellectual rigor and the disciple's yearning for holiness. It answers Elder Neal A. Maxwell's call to explore the book's "divine architecture":

There is so much more in the Book of Mormon than we have yet discovered. The book's divine architecture and rich furnishings will increasingly unfold to our view, further qualifying it as "a marvelous work and a wonder." (Isaiah 29:14) . . . All the rooms in this mansion need to be explored, whether by valued traditional scholars or by those at the cutting edge. Each plays a role, and one LDS scholar cannot say to the other, "I have no need of thee."[1] (1 Corinthians 12:21)

For some time, faithful scholars have explored the book's textual history, reception, historicity, literary quality, and more. This series focuses particularly on theology—the scholarly practice of exploring a scriptural text's implications and its lens on God's work in the world. Series volumes invite Latter-day Saints to discover additional dimensions of this treasured text but leave to prophets and apostles their unique role of declaring its definitive official doctrines. In this case, theology, as opposed to authoritative doctrine, relates to the original sense of the term as, literally, reasoned "God talk." The word also designates a well-developed academic field, but it is the more general sense of the term that most often applies here. By engaging each scriptural book's theology on its own terms, this series explores the spiritual and intellectual force of the ideas appearing in the Latter-day Saints' "keystone" scripture.

Series authors and editors possess specialized professional training that informs their work but, significantly, each takes Christ as theology's proper end because he is the proper end of all scripture and all reflection on it. We, too, "talk of Christ, we rejoice in Christ, we preach of Christ ... that our children may know to what source they may look for a remission of their sins" (2 Nephi 25:26). Moreover, while experts in the modern disciplines of philosophy, theology, literature, and history, series authors and editors also work explicitly within the context of personal and institutional commitments both to Christian discipleship and to the Church of Jesus Christ of Latter-day Saints. These volumes are not official Church publications but can be best understood in light of these deep commitments. And because we acknowledge that scripture demands far more than intellectual experimentation, we call readers' attention to the processes of conversion and sanctification at play on virtually every scriptural page.

Individual series authors offer unique approaches but, taken together, they model a joint invitation to readers to engage scripture in her or his own way. No single approach to theology or scriptural interpretation commands preeminence in these volumes. No volume pretends to be the final word on theological reflection for its part of the Book of Mormon. Varied perspectives and methodologies are evident throughout. This is intentional. In addition, though we recognize love for the Book of Mormon is a "given" for most Latter-day Saint readers, we also share the conviction that, like the gospel of Jesus Christ itself, the Book of Mormon is inexhaustible.[2] These volumes invite readers to slow down and read scripture more thoughtfully and transformatively. Elder Maxwell cautioned against reading the Book of Mormon as "hurried tourists" who scarcely venture beyond "the entry hall."[3] To that end, we dedicate this series to his apostolic conviction that there is always more to learn from the Book of Mormon and much to be gained from our faithful search for Christ in its pages.

—The Editors

Contents

Introduction

If Latter-day Saints know anything in the Book of Mormon well, it's 1 Nephi. We begin there when we start the book over, fresh and excited and committed. Sadly, it's often the only book we get through before our diligence flags—because we stop reading entirely or because we stop reading attentively. But our familiarity with 1 Nephi benefits from this pattern. We know this book best. And so we turn the departure from Jerusalem into novels. We paint the tree of life. We film the trek through the desert. We sing about building the boat. We sermonize about our personal Liahonas. We make keychains that look like the iron rod. Our children strive to be like Nephi. We pray over our Lamans and Lemuels. First Nephi inspires and gives shape to Latter-day Saint devotion.

We also find in 1 Nephi things to think hard about. Some readers revel in the book's preachings about choice lands, its prophecies of Spirit-driven Gentile voyages, and its predictions of latter-day deliverance in battle. Other readers worry about the general invisibility of the women in the book, wonder whether Nephi deserves his brothers' resentment, and lose sleep over the circumstances of Laban's death. Our scholars compile parallels to Lehi's vision of God on his throne and survey the Arabian peninsula tracking Lehi's journey. Some scour the libraries looking for Isaiah's context and meaning. 1 Nephi shapes our thinking as much as our devotion.

But despite our general familiarity with 1 Nephi, we're not yet really acquainted with it. When Elder

Neal A. Maxwell laments that "like hurried tourists" we "scarcely venture beyond the entry hall" of the Book of Mormon, we should probably think of the entry hall as 1 Nephi itself.[1] The problem with such hurried tourism, though, isn't just that it keeps us from getting past 1 Nephi into the rest of the book. It's that it acquaints us just enough with 1 Nephi that, when we're ready to read the Book of Mormon seriously, we're already bored with the first book. We feel we already know the entry hall well, and we hurry past it, never *really* getting to know it. And so, we're all far less familiar with 1 Nephi than we think. It's true we're deeply affected and influenced by this book, but it's true also that we don't tend to take it seriously on its own terms.

My first purpose in the following pages is therefore to show how much we miss in 1 Nephi—how much we miss that's of a theological nature. Even seasoned readers of 1 Nephi usually miss its careful organization and overarching plan, overlook the central focus of its visions and prophecies, and pay too little note to how it talks about God and his work. To give serious attention to these aspects of 1 Nephi is to ask about the book's own spiritual purposes, explicit and implicit. What is the book really after or up to? What does its organization suggest about its aims? What do the book's doctrinal statements claim about divine things? And what do its more subtle emphases and accents say about its worldview?

I respond to these questions in the first half of this book, where I attempt to sort out 1 Nephi's overarching theological project. Chapter 1 considers how 1 Nephi is organized and what this tells us about the book's purposes. Chapter 2 then looks more closely at one of these purposes, which is to explain the history and redemption of Lehi's children. This requires clarifying not only Lehi's and Nephi's prophecies but also Isaiah's. Finally, chapter 3 turns to the other of 1 Nephi's major purposes, which is to clarify the nature of the God who watches over Lehi's children. Because these must "come to the knowledge of the true Messiah" (1 Ne. 10:14), it's crucial to see how the book understands Father, Son, and Holy Ghost.

These are things we begin to notice if we pause in the Book of Mormon's entry hall to take in its actual structure and beauty, if we look for what its designer meant us to experience in its welcoming space. But we're likely to have questions as we gaze at the room's decor. And we likely have questions from our previous, hurried visits too. We mustn't shout out our questions too quickly, silencing the text with clamorous demands for information. But once we've heard 1 Nephi speak in its own voice—once we've experienced the entry hall as intended—we ought to ask our questions and address our concerns. In my experience, we're likely to receive better answers if we've first become genuinely familiar with the room.

What questions are most pressing right now, two decades into the twenty-first century? On this point, I'll take the students in my actual classrooms as guides (I teach courses in religious education at Brigham Young University). What worries them as they read? Do they have concerns for which a theological reading might provide help? I've referred already to readers who worry about the invisibility of the women, wonder whether Nephi deserves his brothers' resentment, and lose sleep over the circumstances of Laban's death. The number of these readers in my classes grows every year. And these questions are essential. They deserve a serious response.

Hence the second half of this book focused on *our* questions about 1 Nephi. Chapter 4 addresses the slaying of Laban. I'll neither justify nor criticize Nephi's actions (or the Spirit's command) but show how the text resists easy answers as it weaves a complex narrative. Chapter 5 then considers Nephi's difficult relationship with his brothers. Here again, I'll neither defend Nephi's brothers nor justify Nephi but rather raise questions about every over-sure reading of the text. Finally, chapter 6 focuses on 1 Nephi's women, so close to invisible in the narrative. That chapter will consider the changing fortunes of women as 1 Nephi develops and once more complicate too-hasty assumptions about Nephi.

There's a pattern to the questions we tend to have about 1 Nephi. They all focus on how the prophet Nephi interacts with nonprophetic characters. He appreciatively inherits the prophetic mantle from his father, but his relationships with everyone else in his story are complicated. To reflect on how Nephi tells his story and offers his prophecies is thus also to reflect on what it means for a prophet to be a prophet. So, while chapters 1–3 delightedly feast on the fruits of the prophet Nephi, chapters 4–6 soberly ask how such delicious fruit comes from such a complicated tree. What I'll emphasize, though, is that it's Nephi himself who tells us just how complicated he is. He doesn't hide the difficulty of his story even as he produces some of the Book of Mormon's most remarkable prophetic material. And this might be the truest sign of true prophecy: that it comes through those God exalts despite their human nature.

First Nephi is more than worthy to open the book of scripture that triggered the Restoration. It weaves the heights of heavenly prophetic rapture into the depths of earthly human experience. Precisely for this reason, it's an astonishing textual embodiment of grace. First Nephi sets up all the problems that plague Lehi's children through the remainder of the Book of Mormon, but it also establishes the high-water mark for the flood of revelation released by the Nephite prophets. 1 Nephi reminds us that "we have this treasure in earthen vessels" (2 Cor. 4:7). It also reminds us that nothing "shall be able to separate us from the love of God" (Rom. 8:39).

PART I

The Theological Project of 1 Nephi

1

Occasion and Structure

We're always missing the big picture because we get stuck on the details. One little aspect of a situation stands out to us for whatever reason, and we end up missing everything else. It's like becoming obsessed with just one scene in a movie and never really getting the point of the whole film. It's not that there isn't anything genuinely interesting about what draws our attention. It's usually quite meaningful, in fact. But we're always missing the bigger picture. And our experience of the world is poorer for it . . .

authors and intentions

The Bible begins with the aptly named book of Genesis. Genesis in turn begins with an executive summary of God's creative activity: "In the beginning God created the heaven and the earth" (Gen. 1:1). Despite traditional claims about authorship, readers aren't sure whose voice they're hearing when they read these words. Who was there to witness God's work of creation? Did someone have a vision of this event? Or is the vertigo the verse induces deliberate? Are we supposed to feel a bit at sea, lost in the "darkness" that "was upon the face of the deep" at the beginning (verse 2)? But then why should we believe these words? Who's romantic enough to trust an announcement from nowhere about the beginning of everything?

Whatever we think about the Bible's opening words, the Book of Mormon's opening words are a study in contrast.[1] First Nephi famously opens with a pronoun and a name: "I, Nephi." This introduces a brief autobiographical sketch of the book's author, one "born of goodly parents" who'd "seen many afflictions" but had "a great knowledge of the goodness and mysteries of God." The verse ends by explaining that these experiences gave Nephi a reason to write, "Therefore I make a record of my proceedings in my days" (1 Ne. 1:1). Genesis begins outside history, but 1 Nephi begins inside history. Genesis begins with an unexplained voice but 1 Nephi with an autobiographical note. Genesis begins without justifying itself, but 1 Nephi begins with an explanation of the author's credentials and reasons for writing.

It might feel irreverent or impertinent to ask how Genesis took shape, but 1 Nephi directly invites us to reflect on its origins. Introduced to the author right away, we're meant to ask about his motivations and strategies. And so it's most useful that he goes on to identify when and how 1 Nephi and its sequel took shape. The text explains that Nephi began work on some kind of record shortly after arriving in the promised land, a record traditionally called the "large plates" (see 1 Ne. 18:25–19:1). But then Nephi contrasts this first-written record with a later project, the "small plates" of Nephi (see 19:2–4; cf. 9:2–6). It's only much later that the text recounts the circumstances under which Nephi produced these small plates, no earlier than thirty years after he'd left Jerusalem and only once he'd left his brothers and started a colony of his own (see 2 Ne. 5:28–34; cf. 1 Ne. 19:5).

The text makes clear that it's this later, small-plates record we're reading when we take up 1 and 2 Nephi. This means that, despite what readers sometimes assume, 1 Nephi isn't an on-the-ground, in-the-moment report of what happened as Lehi's family traveled from Jerusalem to the promised land. Rather, it's a retelling of events decades after they've occurred, colored by later developments (see 1 Ne. 6:1–6). Nephi wrote about his early clashes with his brothers only after separating himself from them permanently—and, in fact, during a time of "wars and contentions" between the distinct peoples (2 Ne. 5:34). First Nephi is less a report about a family's difficult experiences than an explanation, historical *and* theological, for intertribal conflict between Nephites and Lamanites.

All through 1 Nephi, we trace the ebb and flow of antagonism between Nephi and his brothers. Bad feelings largely subside after the sea crossing; 1 Nephi 19–22 describes Nephi peacefully teaching his brothers in the promised land. But conflict flares up again after Lehi's death in 2 Nephi (see 2 Ne. 4:13–14; 5:1–5). We can read the stories in 1 Nephi as preparing us for this final and fateful reemergence of conflict within Lehi's family, which in turn explains the historical contentions between the two peoples. At any rate, these details are familiar to every reader of the Book of Mormon. What we tend to overlook, however, is the text's *theological* approach to the conflict. It's too easy to assume that 1 Nephi's spiritual message amounts to a recommendation that we follow Nephi's example of staying true and faithful amid opposition. But this misses most of what 1 Nephi (as well as 2 Nephi) has to say about the meaning of the Nephite-Lamanite conflict.

How do we discern the text's theological purposes, then? First, we have to ask how 1 Nephi is organized. We're told that Nephi spent decades reflecting on events before he wrote them in the form we encounter them. And he seems to have spent as much as a decade giving shape to the record (see 2 Ne. 5:28, 34). Since Nephi had the time to decide carefully how to compose and to arrange the materials he wished to present, we should expect to find his writings tellingly organized. How does the structure of 1 Nephi relate to theological purpose? Answering this question requires a bit of effort—sorting out the structure of a book of scripture takes work and focus—but it's effort that pays off well in the end.[2]

structure and organization

A first aspect of 1 Nephi's structure is explicitly indicated in the text. Early in chapter 1, Nephi interrupts the story of Lehi's earliest visions to address us as his readers. Worried, it seems, that we might think the book is mostly about Lehi, he explains, "And now I, Nephi, do not make a full account of the things which my father hath written. . . . But I shall make an account of my proceedings in my days" (1 Ne. 1:16–17). This is helpful. But if the real focus is on Nephi's life and story, why begin with so much about Lehi? Nephi continues, "Behold, I make an abridgment of the record of my father . . . ; wherefore, after I have abridged the record of my father then will I make an account of mine own life" (1:17).

This brief editorial interruption explicitly divides 1 Nephi into two distinct parts, two halves. And the dividing line between the two parts is marked later in the text. In the first line of chapter 10, we read, "And now I, Nephi, proceed to give an account upon these plates of my proceedings, and my reign and ministry." These words identify the transition from the abridgment of Lehi's record to Nephi's own "proceedings." Moreover, with the phrase "my reign and ministry," Nephi alludes to the title of this first book ("The First Book of Nephi, His Reign and Ministry"), confirming the transition. In chapters 10–22, it seems, we come to the real core of 1 Nephi, what Nephi's really interested in. Chapters 1–9 apparently provide backstory and context.

It makes good sense to say that 1 Nephi 10–22 contains Nephi's ministry. There we find Nephi's most significant visionary experience (chapters 11–14) and his attempt to explain it to his brothers (chapter 15). There we also find Nephi copying from the brass plates for the first time (chapters 19–21) and attempting to explain them to his brothers (chapter 22). Indeed, apart from the long trek to the promised land (chapters 16–18), the second half of 1 Nephi concentrates solely on Nephi's ministry. Now, from just these details, it's apparent that Nephi's ministry has a double focus and indicates our need to couple past prophecy with present prophecy. Chapters 10–15 find Nephi having and explaining his own prophetic experiences. Chapters 19–22, though, find him reading and explaining the prophetic experiences of Isaiah. The text presents Nephi both as a prophet in his own right, a visionary privileged to see and to teach about sacred history, *and* as a reader of prophets who came before him, interested in understanding and teaching what others have seen in vision. ☞

This first structural detail is interesting, but it's rather broad. Can we get more detailed or more specific about structure in 1 Nephi? We certainly can, but first we need to identify an obstacle to discerning structures in the Book of Mormon. Chapter and verse divisions strongly determine the way we read the text. But such divisions, familiar from recent editions of the Book of Mormon, aren't original to what Joseph Smith dictated to his scribes. In fact, the prophet didn't specify verse or paragraph breaks at all—or even, for that matter, punctuation. He did specify chapter breaks, but they are different from those in recent editions (see FIGURE 1). Looking carefully at original chapters often reveals structural details and helps clarify authorial intent.

☞ Nephi emphasizes this point. He introduces his own vision by affirming that God works through "the power of the Holy Ghost, as well in these times as in times of old" (1 Ne. 10:19). And he opens his quotation of Isaiah with a text that talks of "the former things" spoken by God's servants and of "new things from this time" spoken by the same servants (20:3, 6).

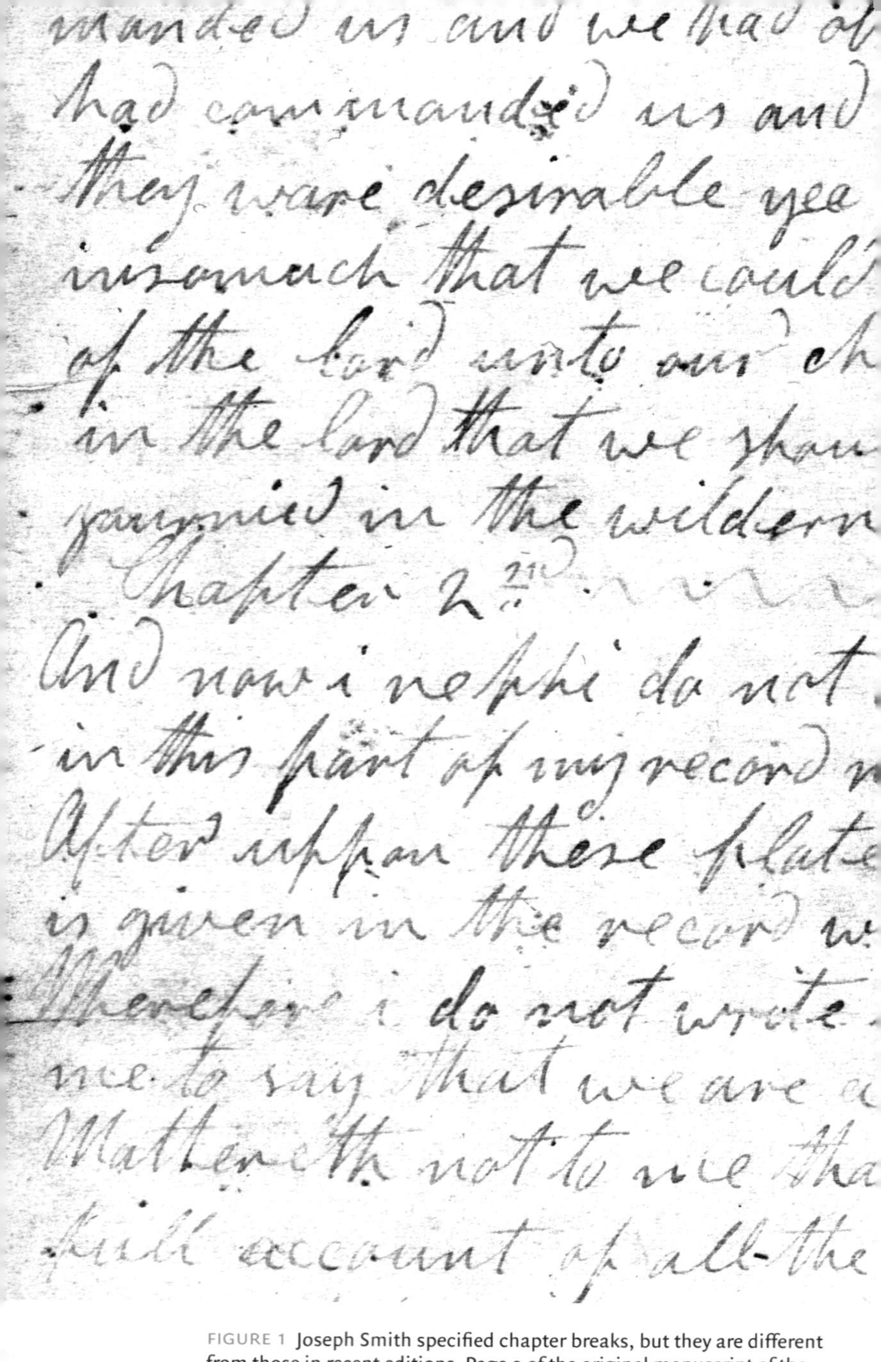
manded us and we had of
had commanded us and
they ware desirable yea
insomuch that we could
of the lord unto our ch
in the land that we shou
journied in the wildern
Chapter 2nd
And now i nephi do not
in this part of my record
After upon these plate
is given in the record w
Therefore i do not write
me to say that we are a
Mattereth not to me tha
full account of all the

FIGURE 1 Joseph Smith specified chapter breaks, but they are different from those in recent editions. Page 9 of the original manuscript of the Book of Mormon, which contains 1 Ne. 5:14–7:3. © Intellectual Reserve, Inc.

...the record which the lord
...ht them and found that...
...i of great worth unto us
...serve the commandments
...n wherefore it was wisdo...
...ry them with us as we
...oward the land of promi...

...the genealogy of my fath
...er at any time shall i give it
...ich i am writing for it
...has bee kept by my fath
...this work for it contin...
...ents of joseph and it
...in particular to give a
...gs of my father for the

Because we'll see that 1 Nephi's structure depends heavily on original chaptering, it's useful to begin with it in mind.³ The original chapters are longer than the ones we know, so they take some getting used to. Here they are (Roman numerals indicate original chapters and Arabic numerals current chapters, see FIGURE 2):

PART 1   **Abridgment of Lehi's Record**

Chapter I = 1 Nephi 1–5
Lehi's First Visions, Departure from Jerusalem, Return for the Pla

Chapter II = 1 Nephi 6–9
Second Return for Ishmael's Family, the Dream of the Tree of Lif

PART 2   **Nephi's Own Proceedings, Reign, and Ministry**

Chapter III = 1 Nephi 10–14
Nephi's Long Vision of Israel's History

Chapter IV = 1 Nephi 15
Nephi's Explanation of his Father's Dream to his Brothers

Chapter V = 1 Nephi 16:1–19:21
Desert Trek, Building a Ship, Ocean Voyage, Prophecies

Chapter VI = 1 Nephi 19:22–21:26
Quotation of Brass Plates Prophecies: Isaiah 48–49

Chapter VII = 1 Nephi 22
Nephi's Explanation of Isaiah to his Brothers

FIGURE 2

What can we learn from 1 Nephi's original chapter breaks? We've already seen the basic shape of Nephi's ministry, the second half of 1 Nephi, but the original chapter breaks make it clearer still. Chapter III contains in one solid block the whole of Nephi's prophetic vision, just as chapter VI presents Nephi's first serious quotation of Isaiah as a unit. And each of these two original chapters is followed by an original chapter where Nephi explains these prophetic visions to his questioning brothers. Chapter IV has him explaining his own vision, and chapter VII has him explaining Isaiah's vision. Finally, chapter V gathers into one continuous narrative the whole journey from Jerusalem to the promised land. The double focus of Nephi's ministry is visible here, and it's neatly divided by the travel narrative.

What of the first half of 1 Nephi, the abridgment of Lehi's record? Nephi apparently abridges Lehi's record into just two parts, chapters I and II. Of course, much can be found in these two chapters: Lehi's first visions and the family's departure from Jerusalem, introductions to the spiritual states of Lehi's sons, the return to Jerusalem for the brass plates, the return to Jerusalem for Ishmael's family, and the famous dream of the tree of life. Nephi groups all of this, though, into just two blocks of text, as if they amounted to just two overarching stories. Seen that way, 1 Nephi 1–9 focuses us on the following two major events: the recovery of the brass plates from Jerusalem (the central story of chapter I) and Lehi's reception of the dream of the tree (the central story of chapter II).

This makes perfect sense in light of the double focus of Nephi's ministry in chapters III–VII. Chapter I explains how Nephi's family came to possess one of the two prophetic resources Nephi uses in his ministry: the brass plates (which is the focus of chapters VI–VII). And chapter II explains how they came to possess the other prophetic resource key to Nephi's ministry: the dream of the tree (which is the focus of chapters III–IV). Thus, in summary, the abridgment of Lehi's record apparently serves in 1 Nephi primarily to explain where the two prophetic resources central to Nephi's reign and ministry came from.

All of this allows us to see the total organization of 1 Nephi (see FIGURE 3). It turns out that 1 Nephi has a tight, deliberate structure. The first half of the book prepares for the second by explaining how Nephi's family came

PART 1 **Abridgment of Lehi's Record:**
Provenance of Key Prophetic Resources

Chapter I (1 Nephi 1–5)
The Provenance of the Brass Plates (Isaiah)

Chapter II (1 Nephi 6–9)
The Provenance of the Dream of the Tree of Life

PART 2 **Nephi's Own Proceedings, Reign, and Ministry:**
Ministerial Use of Key Prophetic Resources

Chapter III (1 Nephi 10–14)
Nephi Himself Experiences the Dream

Chapter IV (1 Nephi 15)
Nephi Explains the Dream to His Brothers

Chapter VI (1 Nephi 19:22–21:26)
Nephi Reads from the Brass Plates (Isaiah)

Chapter VII (1 Nephi 22)
Nephi Explains the Plates (Isaiah) to His Brothers

FIGURE 3

Chapter III—Nephi's Vision on Its Own

Chapter IV—Vision Explained Using Isaiah's Prophecies

—

Chapter VI—Isaiah's Prophecies on Their Own

Chapter VII—Prophecies Explained Using Nephi's Vision

FIGURE 4

to possess the two key prophetic resources essential to Nephi's own subsequent ministerial efforts. The second half of the book then recounts Nephi's ministry to his brothers, built on parallel expositions of the two key prophetic resources from the first half of the book. ☞

theological purpose

In light of 1 Nephi's structure, its theological center of gravity becomes clear. It's the pair of prophetic texts in the book's second half: Nephi's visionary expansion of his father's dream (chapter III) and the block of Isaiah's prophecies (chapter VI). Closer inspection further reveals that Nephi deeply intertwines these two texts (see FIGURE 4). When he explains his father's dream to his brothers after having experienced it himself, he identifies a key resource for explaining it: "I did rehearse unto them the words of Isaiah" (1 Ne. 15:20). Later, when Nephi answers questions about Isaiah, he repeatedly draws on his own vision to explain the prophet's meaning (see 22:6–29). Thus the explanatory chapters

☞ Some might wonder whether the original chapters go back to Nephi. Careful study shows that they do. The original chapters I and II of 1 Nephi, for instance, use the ancient literary device of *inclusio* (bookending a block of text with similar material) to alert readers that they're whole units. Thus the original chapter I opens and closes with parallel stories about a book brought to Lehi that fills him with the Spirit and prompts him to prophesy. And the original chapter II opens and closes with parallel editorial notes that describe the relationship between the small plates and other records in Nephi's collection.

IV and VII, which follow the key prophetic chapters III and VI, respectively, both work to connect Nephi's vision to Isaiah and Isaiah to Nephi's vision. As Nephi says later, "The words of Isaiah are plain unto all those that are filled with the spirit of prophecy" (2 Ne. 25:4).

Nephi has a technical term for the relationship between his vision and Isaiah's writings. It's familiar to readers of the book: *likening*. In the famous verses that open chapter VI (where Nephi first quotes Isaiah), he says this about his interactions with his brothers: "I did read unto them that which was written by the prophet Isaiah; for I did liken all scriptures unto us, that it might be for our profit and learning" (1 Ne. 19:23). Today we generally assume that Nephi here recommends reading scripture with an eye to everyday application. But in context, the text means that Nephi worked to draw out a comparison (a *likeness*) between prophecies he found in Isaiah regarding Jewish history and prophecies he himself set forth regarding the history and fate of Lehi's children (see FIGURE 5).

This is apparent in the next lines of the text. They contain Nephi's introduction to Isaiah, addressed to his brothers: "Hear ye the words of the prophet, ye who are a remnant of the house of Israel, a branch who have been broken off; hear ye the words of the prophet, which were written unto all the house of Israel, and liken them unto yourselves, that ye may have hope as well as your brethren from whom ye have been broken off" (verse 24). The focus of likening here is definitely on the future, and it is explicitly comparative. Likening

Isaiah's Prophecies
History and Destiny of Jews $\longleftarrow$ likening $\longrightarrow$ **Nephi's Vision** History and Destiny of Lehi's Children

FIGURE 5

is about recognizing similarities between the history of the main body of Israel and the histories of its scattered branches. For the most part, then, Isaiah's prophecies aren't for Nephi about everyday faithful living. They're about the long-term destiny of Israel. In Isaiah is a prophetic outline of history that helps to explain what Nephi saw in vision about his own people's future.

All of this indicates that 1 Nephi isn't meant to be primarily a collection of illustrative stories, vignettes modeling faith amid adversity. We're free to read it that way, and maybe we're right to see what we can learn by reading it that way. But Nephi asks us to read his work primarily in a different way. The stories provide context, while we're meant to look for the book's *prophetic* message. And it's clear already from this sketch that that prophetic message especially concerns the destiny of Lehi's children. What Nephi sees in vision, and what he likens Isaiah's prophecies to, is what will happen to latter-day Lamanites. Even when 1 Nephi tells us a didactic story like the one about getting the brass plates, it's also and more centrally introducing us to the scriptural texts from which we'll learn the real meaning of Nephi's visions.

In some ways, moreover, 1 Nephi works like a handbook for 2 Nephi. It introduces us to the two prophetic resources central to Nephi's ministry in the second half of 1 Nephi. But in the same way, it introduces us to what 2 Nephi is all about. The sequel contains long expositions of Isaiah, seen through the lens of Nephi's visions. Perhaps we're baffled and bored by 2 Nephi simply because we're uncareful readers of 1 Nephi. If 1 Nephi can train us to liken, 2 Nephi's obsession with Isaiah will seem natural and exciting rather than unnatural and obnoxious. First Nephi, it seems, is meant to give readers the stamina to follow 2 Nephi's deep and sustained treatment of Israel's divine destiny.

To turn from structure to details, then, we have to ask how 1 Nephi explains what we usually call the Abrahamic covenant. It's in its message regarding Israel's history that 1 Nephi does its key work. What can we say about the book's prophetic message regarding Lehi's children?

It's worth pausing on the fact that Nephi so carefully orders and organizes his record. Maybe it shows us that he's a tidier thinker than we tend to assume. And maybe it shows us that he took real advantage of the time he had to think about the meaning of his experiences. But what it especially shows us, I think, is that Nephi has purposes we ought to let guide us. That's perhaps something we don't often reflect on as we read scripture. We read a little every day, mostly looking for something to touch us, to speak to our everyday life in a way that will help us press on as disciples of Jesus Christ. And there's of course nothing wrong with that. But if it's *all* we do with scripture, we're likely to find that we've silenced the voices of the prophets. Part of what it means to have faith in the prophets is to trust that they have divinely ordained reasons for speaking to us. They aren't just another means to the end of feeling the Spirit and receiving direction for our lives. They're messengers with things we're supposed to come to understand.

Helpfully, Nephi seems willing to lend us a hand by organizing his record so carefully. And even a brief glance at the structure of 1 Nephi shows that a major part of the message in this book is that we ought to trust in the gift of prophecy. Nephi works hard to set side by side two major prophetic voices—his own, of course, but also that of the biblical prophet Isaiah. It seems he wishes us to see that ancient and modern prophecy, so to speak, are to be trusted together. We're to weave the scriptures we carry with us into the words we hear from living, breathing prophets in our own day. Only then can we see the biggest picture of all concerning what God's doing in the world.

2

The Remnant of Israel

Every four years in Sunday School, we spend a day on the Abrahamic covenant. But it always seems to be the same lesson. The teacher writes a short list of things on the board: "promised land," "large posterity," "priesthood keys," "the Messiah." We all scratch our heads for a bit, wondering what any of this has to do with the difficult work of just getting on in life. The stories about Abraham are mildly interesting, but is it really so important that God made promises to someone thousands of years ago?

Lehi's dream

Among the best-known texts in the Book of Mormon is Lehi's dream in 1 Nephi 8. Because it's forceful and accessible, we find in it a powerful representation of every Christian's journey through life. We tread the path leading to Christ, holding God's iron-strong word as we struggle through the darkness of temptation. Though worldly mockery comes from the great and spacious building, we kneel at the life-giving tree, eating what's "sweet above all that is sweet" (Alma 32:42).

It's a beautiful text and a beautiful interpretation. 1 Nephi's structure complicates things, however.[1] The dream appears within the abridgment of Lehi's record, which, we've seen, is meant primarily to explain where Nephi got the sources for his later ministry. Lehi's dream is therefore chiefly a precursor to Nephi's vision in 1 Nephi 10–14. That's no surprise. Most readers recognize a relationship between Lehi's dream and Nephi's vision. Nephi asks to see "the things that [his] father had seen" (11:1), and he does. Along the way, moreover, he explains the dream: what the tree represents, what the mists of darkness signify, what the building means, and so on. But although we see connections between dream and vision, we don't often see the most important implications of their close relationship. We regard Lehi's dream as the story of the individual believer's progress toward Christ. But if that's right, then Nephi's vision isn't about the same thing, because Nephi's vision is about world history, not the individual believer. He witnesses the life of the Messiah, the history of the Nephites, the arrival of Europeans in the Americas, the troubles faced by latter-day Christianity, the coming forth of the Book of Mormon, and the final gathering of Israel. Just how related are these two prophetic experiences, in the end?

It seems important that Lehi, after he "had made an end of speaking the words of his dream" (10:1), goes on immediately to give a sermon (see verses 2–14) that sketches the same history covered in Nephi's vision. In fact, this sermon is the introduction to Nephi's vision, opening the long original chapter (chapter III) in which the vision appears. What's the relationship between Lehi's dream and Lehi's sermon? Some conclude that Lehi distinguishes two things that Nephi's vision then fuses into one: the individual believer's redemption (the dream) and Israel's national redemption (the sermon).[2] But a closer reading suggests that Lehi's dream is about more than the individual believer's redemption.

Every reader of the Book of Mormon knows the dream of the tree of life. We not only tell and retell the story of the dream, we draw it on chalkboards and paint it on canvases. But the dream provides no static picture. Features of the dreamscape emerge one at a time, each coming into focus only at the appropriate moment— precisely as in a dream. But because we try to take in the whole dream at once, we tend to miss something crucial about it. In the dream's first half, there's no talk of iron rods, narrow paths, dark mists, or strange buildings. It's only when Lehi sees "numberless concourses of people" that the way to the tree becomes difficult (8:21). Lehi himself simply runs to the tree when he sees it, heedless of dangerous rivers and imposing buildings, without a path or a rod to guide him. When he beckons to Sariah, also, and to Sam and Nephi, he says nothing of dangers and sources of assistance; he simply calls them to the tree. And although Laman and Lemuel refuse to come and eat, it seems they too could have come without hindrance. The whole family of Lehi apparently has ready access to what subsequent multitudes work hard (and often fail) to reach.

What marks the break between the easier experience of Lehi's family and the more difficult experience of the multitudes? The turning point (see FIGURE 6) in the dream is the moment when Laman and Lemuel "would not come . . . and partake of the fruit" (verse 18). It's at that moment that Lehi says he saw "a rod of iron" and

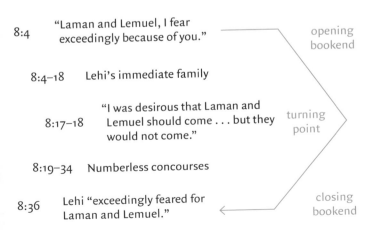

8:4   "Laman and Lemuel, I fear exceedingly because of you."   opening bookend

8:4–18   Lehi's immediate family

8:17–18   "I was desirous that Laman and Lemuel should come . . . but they would not come."   turning point

8:19–34   Numberless concourses

8:36   Lehi "exceedingly feared for Laman and Lemuel."   closing bookend

FIGURE 6

"a strait and narrow path" and "numberless concourses" (verses 19–21). Might the sudden shift in the dream-scape, specifically when Laman and Lemuel refuse the tree, mean that the numberless concourses are the children of Laman and Lemuel—perhaps especially in the last days? Details show that the dream is primarily about Lehi's two oldest sons. The dream account begins with Lehi expressing his "fear" for them (verse 4), and it closes with a parallel expression of fear (see verse 36). The sons' refusal of the fruit comes at the center of the dream account, moreover. Further, the larger original chapter II within which the dream appears (now 1 Ne. 6–9) introduces it by telling of Laman and Lemuel's rebellion in the desert (see 7:6–21). The whole purpose of the dream seems to be to reflect on the long-term implications of what's taking shape within Lehi's family: the budding rebellion of his two oldest sons. In fact, right at the outset of the dream account, Lehi says he's thinking about the long term. He says that the dream is about his sons "and also many of their seed" (8:3).

We're accustomed to thinking that the second half of Lehi's dream is about all human beings striving to find Christ. But there's reason to think that we're meant to see it as a representation of difficulties faced at specific points in history by specific peoples. When the family gives way to numberless concourses of people, it seems it's the seed of Lehi's sons we're reading about—and especially of those sons who have just rejected the tree. Latter-day Lamanites must hold the iron rod (the Book of Mormon) and follow the path (the gospel of Jesus Christ) as they avoid the dangers of the great and spacious building (the Gentiles' great and abominable church). Already in the first half of 1 Nephi, Lehi's dream subtly points to a deep concern for the history and destiny of Lehi's children in the latter days—for those Nephi calls the remnant of Israel (see 13:33–34). We're certainly free to read 1 Nephi 8 as an allegory for our individual struggles to prove faithful. But however we read the chapter, it seems Nephi saw it as a rich embodiment of covenantal history. At any rate, the theme of covenantal history comes out with much greater force in the second half of 1 Nephi. When Nephi begins to prophesy more plainly than Lehi, the meaning of the prophecies in 1 Nephi comes out in stark clarity.

Nephi's vision

Yearning to share his father's visions and "believing that the Lord was able to make them known," Nephi is soon "caught away in the Spirit of the Lord" (1 Ne. 11:1). Before the vision begins, however, Nephi has a remarkable exchange with the Spirit. The Spirit promises a vision of the tree. But then he provides Nephi with a preview of a vision beyond the tree, something like a trailer for the film Nephi is about to watch. "And behold this thing shall be given unto thee for a sign," the Spirit says, "that after thou hast beheld the tree which bore the fruit which thy father tasted, thou shalt also behold a man descending out of heaven, and him shall ye witness; and after ye have witnessed him ye shall bear record that it is the Son of God" (verse 7). This promise, which immediately precedes the vision, presumably sets up expectations for Nephi. It certainly should do so for us as readers. We're meant to go into our reading of Nephi's vision watching for the descent of the Son of God from heaven.

Ironically, though, when Nephi gets his first glimpse of the Son of God, Christ isn't descending out of heaven. Nephi sees him first cradled in the Virgin's arms and then watches as this "Lamb of God" (verse 21) goes to be baptized, ministers among the people, receives angelic visitors, and heals the afflicted. Finally,

Nephi sees "the Lamb of God, that he was taken by the people" and "lifted up upon the cross" (verses 32–33). Readers track the Messiah's life and death without a hint of what we've been promised we'll see: a vision of the Son of God's descent from heaven. In fact, the promised event doesn't come until after the Messiah's death, when the scene changes from first-century Jerusalem to first-century America. After "many generations" of "wars and contentions" in the promised land, Nephi finally sees "the heavens open, and the Lamb of God descending out of heaven" (12:3, 6). It turns out that the Spirit has pointed Nephi not to Jesus Christ's mortal mission but rather to his exalted visit to Lehi's children recorded in 3 Nephi.

As Christians, this might leave us surprised. We might expect the life, ministry, and death of Jesus of Nazareth to be the heart of Nephi's film-like vision. But the trailer for this film has directed Nephi and us to something beyond those exalted events, as if the New Testament were really just the backstory to the central drama. First Nephi 11 is preparatory to 1 Nephi 12, an anticipation of or an introduction to the real focus of Nephi's vision. Is it irreverent to make Christ's mortal ministry part of the stage setting rather than the main event? But isn't it appropriate that Nephi would see Jesus's mortal life as a preface to his immortal descent among Israelites in the promised land? Nephi's prophetic priorities aren't our own. In the world's history as he witnesses it, the first key moment in the Lamb's work occurs when he visits the remnant of Israel in the New World. ☞

☞ It's worth noting that, although Nephi mentions Christ's crucifixion, he says nothing directly about either Christ's atonement or his resurrection. The last detail is perhaps particularly surprising. The story of Christ's mortal advent ends, in Nephi's vision, not with victory over death but with Israel fighting against Christ's apostles.

31

The Spirit's Trailer to the Film (1 Ne. 11:7)

"Thou shalt also behold a man descending out of heaven, and . . . ye shall bear record that it is the Son of God."

The Film's First Sequence (1 Ne. 11:11–36)

The life and death of Christ without any descent from heaven, preparatory to the anticipated vision of The Second Sequence.

The Second Sequence (1 Ne. 12:1–23)

The anticipated descent of the Lamb among Lehi's children, though it's over quickly, leaving open questions about Lamanite redemption.

The Third Sequence (1 Ne. 13:1–14:17)

The story of Lamanite redemption, involving latter-day Gentiles.

FIGURE 7

Unfortunately, the peaceful results of the Lamb's visit to Lehi's children last only a few generations before "wars and rumors of wars" resume and Nephi sees his seed overpowered and destroyed (1 Ne. 12:21). After so much build-up, what this film's trailer has led Nephi and us to anticipate as the climax passes too quickly, and we're left disoriented (see FIGURE 7). We're confronted with unexpected tragedy in that the descent of the Son of God hasn't solved all the problems, and we wonder whether and how Lehi's surviving children might again come to know the figure who descended out of heaven to minister to them. Thankfully, the rest of Nephi's vision tells the story of how that happens. And so it turns out that, like Lehi's dream, Nephi's vision is about getting the children of Laman and Lemuel into God's presence. And as in Lehi's dream, what's needed is a rod and a path, as well as avoidance of a great and spacious building.

The history Nephi sees next is complex, requiring constant explanation by an angelic guide. It moves quickly through early modern history to the point where the Americas are peopled with Europeans freed from the rule of "their mother Gentiles" (13:17). What draws Nephi's interest the most here, though, is a book carried by the Gentiles settled among Lehi's children, among the remnant of Israel. "I beheld a book," Nephi says, "and it was carried forth among them" (verse 20).

Because Nephi doesn't know the book's "meaning" (verse 21), the angel explains it. It's the Christian Bible, which was in fact key to the self-understanding of early modern Europeans in the New World. But the angel's description of the book is startlingly peculiar. He emphasizes twice that the book is Jewish, and he twice states that it "contains the covenants of the Lord, which he hath made unto the house of Israel" (verse 23). What's so peculiar about this? Through most of Christian history, and certainly in the context of early modern European expansion, Christians have seen the Bible as a Christian (rather than Jewish) book, and they've seldom emphasized the covenants made to Israel (at least as covenants that remain relevant to Israel). Maybe more obviously peculiar is the fact that the angel speaks of prophets in the book but says nothing about apostles—or, in fact, about Jesus Christ! According to the angel, the Christian Bible is first a Jewish book about Israel's covenants. He provocatively adds that this is why the book, perhaps without Christians knowing it, is "of great worth unto the Gentiles" (verse 23).

Why hasn't the Christian world seen the Bible as the angel sees it? The angel answers this question with a long story. At first, the book would contain "the fulness of the gospel of the Lord" as it goes "from the Jews in purity unto the Gentiles" (verses 24–25). But then a "great and abominable church" would cause trouble for the book, having "taken away from the gospel of the

Lamb many parts which are plain and most precious" (verse 26). The angel emphasizes that this transformation of the gospel would be deliberate: "And all this have they done that they might pervert the right ways of the Lord, that they might blind the eyes and harden the hearts of the children of men" (verse 27). Once the gospel has been changed, the book's very contents look different: "Wherefore, thou seest that after the book hath gone forth through the hands of the great and abominable church, that there are many plain and precious things taken away from the book" (verse 28).

We have to be careful with a few things here. For example, despite traditional associations, it's wrong to identify Nephi's great and abominable church with historical Catholicism. The events described by the angel fit better in the first and second centuries than in later history. This would seem to imply that Catholicism and all other branches of Christianity are innocent heirs to (rather than devious inventors of) the problem Nephi's angel describes. Similarly, we have to be careful in making accusations about tampering with the Bible. The angel's description suggests a change in doctrinal framework first ("the gospel") and only subsequently in actual texts ("the book"). It might even be that the texts are supposed to have remained relatively stable, while changes in interpretation have led to misunderstanding. At any rate, we must be careful while asking a crucial question: What exactly is supposed to have gone missing from the gospel so early in Christian history? What are the "plain and precious things" taken away (verse 28)?

We have a key to the meaning of "plain and precious" later in the vision, when Nephi uses it to describe Christ's teachings during his visit to Lehi's children in 3 Nephi (see verse 35). It's telling also that Nephi uses the same phrase to summarize the prophecies

The "Plain and Precious":

1. Taken from the gospel and book of the Lamb
(see 1 Ne. 13:26, 28)

2. Found in the Covenant sermons of Jesus Christ in 3 Nephi
(see 1 Ne. 13:35)

3. Found in the Covenant prophecies of Jacob, Isaiah, and
Nephi in 2 Nephi (see 1 Ne. 19:1–6; 2 Ne. 5:28–34)

FIGURE 8

contained in 2 Nephi 6–30, those of Isaiah, of Nephi's
brother Jacob, and of Nephi himself (see 1 Ne. 19:5).
Because 2 Nephi 6–30 and Christ's sermons in 3 Nephi
both focus on the prophetic history of Israel, it seems
that the "plain and precious things" are whatever must
be understood to see what God is doing in history with
what we call the Abrahamic covenant (see FIGURE 8).
That is, what's supposed to have gone missing in earliest Christianity is, it seems, a full understanding of
Israel's destiny. It's striking that Nephi's angelic guide
directly explains that "many covenants of the Lord have
[the Gentiles] taken away" from the Lamb's gospel
(1 Ne. 13:26). We might initially guess that this means
that early Christians jettisoned specific ordinances
(and thus covenants), but the only covenants mentioned by Nephi and the angel anywhere in the vision
are "the covenants of the Lord, which he hath made
unto the house of Israel" (verse 23). Since these very
covenants are, according to the angel, the focus of the
Bible, it seems that this is what Nephi wishes us to see
as having been lost early in Christian history.

Some kind of removal of the right picture of
the Abrahamic covenant therefore apparently lies at
the foundation of the great and abominable church,
that "strange building" that tempts the remnant and

35

repentant Gentiles away from the truth (8:33). The transformation of the gospel is supposed to have begun early in Christian history.[3] The angel expects it to continue into the modern period as well, troubling "the Gentiles who have gone forth out of captivity" into the promised land (13:30). Incidentally, we can trace in the first centuries of Christian history developments along exactly the lines laid down in the vision: the beginnings of a general forgetting of God's "ancient covenant people," "the travails, and the labors, and the pains of the Jews, and their diligence" (2 Ne. 29:4–5). But, however we understand early Christian history, Nephi's vision places the Bible at the root of religious trouble in the last days. Confusion about its core message trips up the Gentiles who have filled the world with Christianity. And this has devastating consequences for native peoples conquered by Europeans. In the promised land, Gentile religious confusion leaves the shattered Lamanites wary about "the book of the Lamb of God" embraced by their violent conquerors (1 Ne. 13:38). The Gentiles need correction, but it must be done in a way that would allow Lehi's children also to see "that the records of the prophets and of the twelve apostles of the Lamb are true" (verse 39).

The angel assures Nephi that God won't "suffer that the Gentiles shall forever remain in that awful state of blindness" (verse 32). But how to solve the problem so as to serve Israel's remnant as much as misguided Gentiles? The angel quotes the Lamb: "I will bring forth unto [the Gentiles], in mine own power, much of my gospel, which shall be plain and precious" (verse 34). This is to happen, according to the Lamb, through the coming forth of the Book of Mormon (see verses 35–36). The Book of Mormon will be the iron rod that leads latter-day Lamanites—and Gentiles with them—along the gospel path. And so Nephi sees the Book of Mormon's coming forth, prompting Gentile Christians to recognize that Christ manifests himself to *all* nations but also and especially restoring the latter-day remnant of Israel to an understanding of *their* covenantal status. When the Bible and the Book of Mormon are together in the hands of Israel's remnant, they come to know "that the Lamb of God is the Eternal Father, and the Savior of the world; and that all men must come unto him, or they cannot be saved" (verses 38–40).[4] And repentant Gentiles, the angel explains, will join those already in the covenant to become "a blessed people upon the promised land forever" (14:2). Then "the work of the Father shall commence," triggering the final "fulfilling of his covenants, which he hath made to his people who are of the house of Israel" (verse 17).

With the rod-like word in circulation and the path to Christ clear, with Israel knowing its own covenantal identity and gathering with Gentile help, the film-like vision comes at last to an end, and the credits begin to roll. But it takes Nephi some time to gather his wits after such a powerful visual experience. Stumbling back to his father's tent, he finds he has to explain the vision's meaning to his wondering brothers. How could he do so? Nephi tells us he used "the words of Isaiah" (15:20). This seems appropriate since, as we've seen, 1 Nephi's structure indicates that Nephi's vision has its full meaning only side by side with Isaiah's prophecies. We must ask what Nephi finds in Isaiah.

Isaiah's prophecies

Isaiah is the thorn in the side of many a Book of Mormon reader. Nephi tells us, though, that his "soul delighteth in his words" (2 Ne. 11:2). This is evident already in 1 Nephi, where the first substantial quotation of Isaiah appears. This quotation consists of just two chapters (Isa. 48–49) and therefore doesn't slow most readers down. It's the thirteen-chapter block in 2 Nephi that's often called the "Isaiah barrier." Even so, many puzzle over the meaning of the Isaiah chapters that conclude 1 Nephi. What role do they play in the text?[5]

Themes in Isaiah 48 loosely recall circumstances in Lehi's trek through the desert. The text mentions hypocritical trust in Jerusalem, divine prophecy meant to guide Israel, the Lord's care for those who declare his word, seed like the sands of the sea, and divine deliverance in the desert. There's even a reminder that "notwithstanding [the Lord] hath done all this, and greater also, there is no peace . . . unto the wicked" (1 Ne. 20:22). It doesn't take much imagination to tie all these themes to the story of the wilderness journey. But there's more than immediate applicability in Isaiah 48. The prophecy announces restoration of exiled Jews from a situation of oppression and captivity. And it emphasizes that the event of restoration will be entirely accomplished by grace. These are larger historical themes like those in Nephi's vision.

We might be quick to assume that the event of restoration in the Isaiah text is a latter-day affair, that it straightforwardly predicts events we hope to see happen in our own time. But the text makes repeated references to Jews in exile in Babylon during Nephi's own lifetime, six centuries before Christ. Which is it? Is Isaiah interested in ancient or modern events? This is an important question because scholars tend to argue that we should restrict Isaiah's meaning to an ancient context, while lay readers tend to assume that everything in Isaiah points directly to the last days. But are we really meant to choose between these alternatives? Nephi says later that he sees Isaiah's prophecies as having an ancient *and* a latter-day fulfillment (see 2 Ne. 25:9–19). His brother Jacob suggests the same when he says that Isaiah's words concern "things which are," things six centuries before Christ, and things "which are to come," things to happen only much later (6:5). ☞

The theme of promised redemption from exile and oppression continues into Isaiah 49. And it's evidently this theme of redemption that draws Nephi's attention to both chapters. He never suggests a direct application of Isaiah's words to his family's desert sojourn. But Nephi does emphatically connect the two chapters—especially Isaiah 49—to his own prophecies of redemption for Israel. Thus, Isaiah 48 introduces the theme of restoration that's then developed more fully in Isaiah 49. And it's Isaiah 49 that deserves the most attention, because of its detail and specificity, but especially because it's this chapter that Nephi will quote and allude to repeatedly.

Isaiah 49 begins by calling Israel God's secret weapon, "a sharp sword" hidden "in the shadow of [his] hand" (1 Ne. 21:2). But Israel is skeptical, countering that the nation has "labored in vain" and now wallows in exile (verse 4). The Lord's response is to explain his hidden purposes: "It is a light thing that thou shouldst be my servant to raise up the tribes of Jacob, and to restore the preserved of Israel. I will also give thee for a light to the Gentiles, that thou mayest be my salvation unto the ends of the earth" (verse 6). Redeeming Israel is too simple, it seems. The Lord has other purposes in Israel's exile and promised redemption. Israel will apparently be God's secret weapon, then, in the following way: exiled among nations they've failed to reach in their witness of God, Jews will experience a redemption miraculous and spectacular enough to draw Gentile attention. Gentiles will in fact make Israel's grace-filled

☞ The apparent motivation for the idea of double fulfillment is Isaiah 11:11, quoted in context in 2 Nephi 21:11 and alluded to in the small plates by both Nephi and Jacob in 2 Nephi 6:14; 25:17; 29:1 and Jacob 6:2.

restoration happen and in the process come to see that Israel's God *is* God (see Isa. 52:7–10, alluded to in 1 Ne. 13:37; 22:10–11). Jerusalem worries that "the Lord hath forsaken" the covenant people (1 Ne. 21:14), but Gentile "kings" and "queens" will carry Israel's "sons" and "daughters" home (verses 22–23). Persians would do this for Jews in the sixth century before Christ, but so would latter-day Gentiles for Jews scattered across the earth (see 2 Ne. 10:6–9).

Despite appearances, what Nephi finds in these Isaiah texts is a simple story. Like the prophets at the time of Lehi (see 1 Ne. 1:4), Isaiah predicts that Jerusalem would be destroyed and many of its surviving inhabitants carried into exile. But like Lehi after his escape into the desert (see 10:3), Isaiah predicts also that Babylon would fall while Gentiles would exemplify God's graceful care for the covenant people, carrying them home and joining in their faith. This is the simple pattern in these chapters of Isaiah, and Nephi apparently sees it occurring twice in history—once six centuries before Christ (redemption from exile in Babylon) and once at the end of history (final redemption for scattered Jews generally).

The pattern (and associated history) seems simple enough, then. But why should Nephi be interested in it? In Isaiah, it concerns only and explicitly the portion of Israel that Lehi's family has left behind: "the Jews who were at Jerusalem" (1 Ne. 2:13). Nephi's concern is a different Israelite people, settled in the New World. It's here, though, that likening is essential. Nephi's last words before quoting Isaiah are, "Hear ye the words of the prophet, which were written unto all the house of Israel, and liken them unto yourselves, that ye may have hope as well as your brethren from whom ye have been broken off" (19:24). Something in Isaiah is *like* what Nephi sees in vision regarding Lehi's children. Just as

Isaiah's prophecies give hope to Jews in exile, there's hope for languishing latter-day Lamanites. So what has Nephi's vision to do with Isaiah 48–49?

Isaiah predicts destruction for Israel's wickedness; just a remnant will survive, and only in exile among oppressing Gentiles. But Isaiah then predicts a shift in Israel's situation, with Gentiles becoming Israel's benefactors, caring for and restoring them. This is exactly what Nephi sees in vision but in a parallel Israelite context. Part of New-World Israel, the Nephites, will be destroyed. The Lamanites, a remnant of Israel, will survive but only to find themselves captive to oppressing Gentiles in the early modern period. Nephi too, though, predicts a shift in this remnant of Israel's situation, with New-World Gentiles bringing the Book of Mormon to Lamanites in spiritual exile. And believing Gentiles will work to gather and restore Lehi's children. The two stories, Nephi's and Isaiah's, are one, although occurring among different branches of Israel. Seeing how God deals with one branch of Israel in Isaiah, and likening this to other branches of Israel, one finds hope for all Israel.

It's easy, in the end, to see how Nephi taught his brothers about Lehi's dream and his own vision by reading Isaiah to them. He used texts focused on a political history they knew well, set in a familiar geographical landscape, and addressing divinely orchestrated events on the very near horizon. In this way, Nephi began from what his brothers could readily understand. They could find in Isaiah a familiar story "concerning the restoration of the Jews" (1 Ne. 15:19). And from there, Nephi could extrapolate to what he and his father saw in vision: a far-off history with good news for their own descendants. Nephi doesn't mean any of this to be mystifying but quite down to earth. He of course recognizes that later generations among his people would be left scratching their heads (see 2 Ne. 25:1–2, 4–6). But he also realizes that those "in the last days" can "understand" Isaiah readily, having access to historical sources and geographical information he didn't pass on to his own children (verse 8). And, at any rate, Isaiah only confirms and clarifies—as well as enriches—the patterns of covenant history Nephi outlines in his own vision account.

Of course, covenantal history in Nephi's vision moves toward *two* climactic events. Nephi explains that latter-day Lamanites will "know and come to the knowledge of their forefathers," recognizing their part in Israel's destiny. But he claims also that they will "come to . . . the knowledge of the gospel of their Redeemer, which was ministered unto their fathers by him" (1 Ne. 15:14). It's not only Israel's history that's at stake here, although that's what 1 Nephi emphasizes. It's also Israel's God they must come to know. What, then, might be said about "the very God of Israel" (19:7), as he's understood in 1 Nephi?

Moroni was a close reader of Nephi's writings. He borrows from Nephi's record frequently, much more often than does his father, Mormon. But the place where Moroni's debt to Nephi is clearest is in the title page he provided for the Book of Mormon. Nephi writes that "the Jews" and "the Gentiles" must eventually become "convinced" that "Jesus is the Christ, the Eternal God" (2 Ne. 26:12). Moroni copies this directly into the title page. Nephi writes of Lehi's promise that Laman and

Lemuel would find mercy, that "the Lord would . . . not cast them off" (1 Ne. 8:37). Moroni copies this directly into the title page. Nephi makes these themes central to his own two books, saturating his readers especially with the theme of the Abrahamic covenant, the theme of redemption for the remnant of Israel. But Moroni then asks readers of the whole of the Book of Mormon to look for these same themes beyond their reading of Nephi. He learns from the small plates to make Israel's destiny a focus of intense study, and he invites everyone who opens the Book of Mormon to do the same.

Moroni invites us to read the Book of Mormon with an eye to Israel's redemption. But further, we're ourselves living in the times Nephi saw in vision, when Israel's remnants would be recovered from the four quarters of the earth. The Gentiles have begun their work of seeking Israel's scattered branches all over the world, and recent decades have witnessed the real beginnings of redemption for Lehi's children in particular. We should share Nephi's obsession with the history of the Abrahamic covenant. Perhaps we should even share his obsession with Isaiah. We're living out the things Nephi saw only at a distance. He watched as his brothers wandered from God, but we have the opportunity to work as the descendants of Nephi's brothers come faithfully back. It's not just that Nephi saw our day. He received promises regarding events we're living through, and he may be the best guide we have to understanding the significance of those events.

3

The God of Israel

The Nephites sometimes seem confused about the nature of God. It's clear they knew of Christ centuries before his coming. Their testimonies of the Savior are touching, and their explanations of the atonement are rich and deep. But do they know and teach about the Father? And how do they understand the Holy Ghost? Did they perhaps not have the full truth of God revealed to them? Or is there perhaps something we're supposed to learn from their unwavering focus on the Son? . . .

the baptized Lamb

The first half of 1 Nephi gives way to the second half somewhat hesitantly. No sooner does Nephi announce that he's done abridging his father's record than he pauses to explain, "To proceed with mine account, I must speak somewhat of the things of my father, and also of my brethren" (1 Ne. 10:1). The text thus moves from Lehi's dream to Nephi's vision only after a brief synopsis of a sermon from Lehi (see verses 2–15). A repeating formula ("much spake my father concerning") marks the sermon's core themes, signaling that Nephi leaves much out of his synopsis and indicating what's most central to Lehi's words. Since the synopsis introduces Nephi's vision, the two things Lehi "spake much" about are things Nephi wants us to watch for as the text continues.

Unsurprisingly, one theme is the Abrahamic covenant. "Yea, even my father spake much concerning the Gentiles, and also concerning the house of Israel,"

Nephi says, "that they should be compared like unto an olive tree, whose branches should be broken off and should be scattered upon all the face of the earth" (verse 12). We've seen that this theme is central to Nephi's vision and to all of 2 Nephi. The other theme is more surprising. Lehi spoke much also about "a prophet who should come before the Messiah, to prepare the way of the Lord"—a prophet who cries "in the wilderness," baptizes "in Bethabara," and finally baptizes "the Messiah with water" (verses 7–9). The second theme Nephi wishes to highlight before turning to his own visionary experience is, it seems, the fact that the Messiah would be baptized.

Perhaps we should be unsurprised. Nephi goes on to witness the Messiah's baptism early in his own vision. Also, Nephi's angelic guide lays striking emphasis on the theological significance of this event. "And the angel said unto me again," Nephi reports, "Look and behold the condescension of God! And I looked and beheld the Redeemer of the world, of whom my father had spoken; and I also beheld the prophet who should prepare the way before him. And the Lamb of God went forth and was baptized of him" (11:26–27). Although commentators loosely associate God's condescension with the Messiah's birth, ministry, and death,[1] the angel ties God's condescension to the Messiah's baptism. This lends the latter event a weighty significance. And, of course, Nephi confirms the theological importance of the Messiah's baptism at his record's end. In his final "few words" dedicated to "the doctrine of Christ" (2 Ne. 31:2), Nephi asks readers to remember "that prophet which the Lord showed unto [him], that should baptize the Lamb of God" (verse 4). He comments at length on the meaning of Christ's baptism. Thus, Nephi's own final reflections in his larger record focus on the implications of what Lehi emphasizes in 1 Nephi 10.

The consistent emphasis on this theme deserves reflection. In 2 Nephi, Christ's baptism becomes an "example" for all to follow (2 Ne. 31:9), a model of what's expected "until after [the Messiah] shall manifest himself . . . in the flesh" (32:6). In 1 Nephi, the matter is vaguer, a business of divine condescension. And yet the Messiah's baptism in 1 Nephi introduces readers to a key theological title for the Messiah. Lehi prophesies not only that the Messiah's prophetic forerunner would baptize him but also that this forerunner would "behold and bear record that he had baptized the Lamb of God" (1 Ne. 10:10). The preparatory prophet would thus do more than administer a necessary ordinance. He would see something others wouldn't, and he would bear public witness to it: that the Messiah is God's Lamb. This theologically fraught title—"the Lamb of God"—proves central to Nephi's vision. We'll see that it's the Lamb that lies at the heart of the presentation of Israel's God in 1 Nephi.

"The Lamb of God" is a familiar title for latter-day Christians, but it's uncommon in scripture (see FIGURE 9).

Use of "the Lamb" in Scripture

New Testament	Twice in John 1, twenty-eight times in Revelation
Book of Mormon	Fifty-seven times in 1 Nephi 10–14, four times in 2 Nephi 31–33, four times in Mormon's writings, five times in Moroni's writing
Doctrine and Covenants	Fourteen times
Pearl of Great Price	Once

FIGURE 9

It never appears in the Old Testament. In the New Testament's Gospels, it appears only in John's first chapter, on the lips of the testifying Baptist (see John 1:29, 36). In the rest of the New Testament, it appears only in Revelation, but there it shows up twenty-eight times. As for uniquely Latter-day Saint scripture, Christ is the Lamb in the Doctrine and Covenants and the Pearl of Great Price only in allusions to Revelation. In the Book of Mormon, the title is almost entirely restricted to Nephi's vision. Lehi introduces it in 1 Nephi 10, and then it appears fifty-six times in the course of Nephi's vision, which is explicitly related to John's Revelation (see 1 Ne. 14:18–27). After that, the title mostly disappears. Nephi uses it late in 2 Nephi, referring back to his vision. And then it appears a few times in the remainder of the volume but always mirroring the book of Revelation or the Baptist's words in John.

Thus, references to God's Lamb throughout scripture derive either from the Baptist's testimony or from the apocalyptic visions of John and Nephi. The title is obviously of theological significance, since it presents Christ as a sacrifice in whose blood the repentant are washed white. Although there is disagreement among scholars about exactly which form of Israelite sacrifice (or other cultural traditions) the image derives from, numerous Book of Mormon passages show that it's the blood of the Lamb that's most essential to the Nephite prophets.[2] But "the Lamb" is also an apocalyptic title, that is, an identity that's made clear *only* through a privileged form of revelation. When Israel's God reveals his role in history to chosen vessels like John or Nephi, he presents himself as the Lamb. This is a gesture of condescension.

What Nephi sees in vision regarding the destiny of Lehi's children is principally the story of the Lamb. Christ is the Lamb when Nephi first sees him in the arms of the Virgin (see 1 Ne. 11:21), and he is the Lamb again when Nephi sees him baptized (see verse 27). He's the Lamb in his mortal ministry (see verse 31), and he's the Lamb when he's "judged of the world" and killed (verse 32). He's the Lamb when he descends from heaven to visit Lehi's children (see 12:6), and he's the Lamb when the Nephites write and seal up his teachings (see 13:35). The pure gospel corrupted by the abominable church belongs to the Lamb (see verse 26), as does the pure book that goes from Jews to Gentiles before its corruption (see verse 28). It's also the Lamb who reaches out in mercy in the last days (see verse 33), brings forth the Book of Mormon (see verse 39), and destroys the abominable church (see 14:3). And, of course, it's to the Lamb that "all men must come" in the end, "or they cannot be saved" (13:40). In the vision that forms the theological heart of 1 Nephi, it's the Lamb of God who requires our worship.

Of course, while "the Lamb of God" is the most privileged of Christ's titles in 1 Nephi, and the one with the most obvious theological significance, it's not the only way Nephi refers to the God of Israel. Other terms and titles deepen the meaning of Nephi's presentation of the Lamb.

Messiah and Redeemer

Christ is actually introduced first in 1 Nephi as "the Messiah." When Lehi becomes a prophet in Jerusalem, he announces that his visions have "manifested plainly of the coming of a Messiah, and also the redemption of the world" (1 Ne. 1:19).[3] Lehi seems to be referring to the "One" he saw in a vision, "descending out of the midst of heaven" with twelve attendants and shining with a "luster . . . above that of the sun at noon-day" (verse 9). It's Lehi's talk of "a Messiah" that puts him in danger in Jerusalem, so that he's commanded to leave the city. But he returns to his messianic theme in teaching his sons in the wilderness, in the sermon Nephi summarizes in the transition to the second half of 1 Nephi. After predicting the return of exiled Jews to Jerusalem, Lehi predicts the Messiah's coming. "Yea, even six hundred years from the time that my father left Jerusalem," Nephi reports, "a prophet would the Lord God raise up among the Jews—even a Messiah, or, in other words, a Savior of the world" (10:4). Lehi claims to find this prediction in the writings of the prophets in the brass plates (see verse 5).

Although Lehi goes on in the same sermon to equate the Messiah with the Lamb, he doesn't use the latter title again. In his final teachings, in 2 Nephi 1–4, Lehi still speaks of "the Messiah" (see 1:10; 2:6, 8, 26; 3:5). And up until he reports Lehi's death (except within the account of his long vision), Nephi too seems generally content to speak of "the Messiah" (see 1 Ne. 10:17; 15:13). The consistent use of this title in 1 Nephi, as well as its foundational theological role there, suggests that it helps to determine the meaning of Israel's God in the book. And it's crucial to recognize that Lehi understands the Messiah to be Israel's God. He at first speaks vaguely enough that readers might think the Messiah is just someone sent by God, but Lehi eventually directly identifies the Messiah with Israel's God. This is clearest in 2 Nephi, where Lehi speaks of "the Holy One of Israel, the true Messiah" (2 Ne. 1:10). Already within 1 Nephi, however, Nephi identifies the Messiah with "the Son of God" (1 Ne. 10:17) and even with the "Lord" and the "Redeemer" (verse 14).

What does it mean to speak of Israel's God as the Messiah? In the biblical context, this means something specific. The word *messiah* transliterates a Hebrew term that means, simply, "anointed." It's used in the Old Testament to refer to kings and priests, those anointed to reign or to minister. But because Israel faced prolonged periods of deep disappointment regarding their kings and priests, and because Israel's prophets repeatedly spoke of better things to come, there developed a strong sense of anticipation for a divinely sent king or priest (or a king-and-priest) who would set things right. Further, Israel had a responsibility to the nations, the task of teaching them the true God. But because Israel spent much of its ancient history crushed by political foes, the prophets spoke of how a true king and priest might deliver them from enemies and lead them in bringing the nations to true knowledge about God. To speak of the Messiah in the biblical context is thus to speak of specific forms of anticipation.[4]

Should we assume this backdrop for 1 Nephi? Nephi doesn't at first explain the meaning of the title "the Messiah" for his readers. But his brother Jacob later states that the Messiah is a figure Jews "wait for" (2 Ne. 6:13), and Nephi himself eventually notes that the Messiah is a figure Jews "look forward . . . for" (25:18). Further, already in 1 Nephi, references to the Messiah often appear alongside the verb *come*, and the fuller title, "the Messiah, who should come," appears twice (1 Ne. 10:11, 17). Thus, for 1 Nephi, as for the Bible, to speak of the Messiah is to speak of the future and of anticipation. It's also therefore to speak of the incompleteness and brokenness of how things are at present. Lehi's first references to the Messiah refer not only to his "coming" but also to "the redemption of the world" (1:19). "The Messiah" is a name as much for New-World as for Old-World Israel's deeply felt need to see things finally fixed. The Nephites, like the Israelites they left behind in Jerusalem, long for healing because the world is wounded. They look forward. They wait.

Nephi's vision in 1 Nephi 10–14, however, gets specific about this waiting in a way that's foreign to the

Old Testament prophets. He predicts the Virgin's role in the Messiah's birth (see 11:19–20). He names the tiny first-century village where the Messiah will grow to adulthood (see verse 13). He describes the Messiah's baptism and names the location of its occurrence (see 11:27; 10:9). He outlines the Messiah's ministry and how it will provoke violence (see 11:28–32). He identifies the peculiar Roman institution—crucifixion—that will be used to execute the Messiah (see verse 33). He even provides a rough date for these occurrences (see 10:4). Nephi doesn't wait vaguely for redemption; he looks forward to quite specific events, with astonishing precision. Nothing like this level of specificity can be found in the Old Testament. And so Nephi explicitly notes that the "plainness" of his own prophecies distinguishes them from those in the Bible (see 2 Ne. 25:4). This seems to be why he claims that "there is none other people that understand the things which were spoken unto the Jews" by their own Old Testament prophets "save it be that they are taught after the manner of the things of the Jews" (verse 25). Even then, it seems Nephi thinks that most Israelites didn't understand the teachings of their prophets. Old-World Israelites knew of lambs and messiahs, but Nephi claims they seldom looked to the Lamb or the Messiah with any real clarity.

It thus seems important that Nephi eventually provides a prophecy in which he predicts the name of the Messiah: "For according to the words of the prophets, the Messiah cometh in six hundred years from the time that my father left Jerusalem; and according to the words of the prophets, and also the word of the angel of God, his name shall be Jesus Christ, the Son of God" (2 Ne. 25:19). This mirrors a revelation by Nephi's brother Jacob, recorded also in 2 Nephi, in which the name of the Messiah is revealed as "Christ" (10:3). Such revelations, though, aren't relegated solely to 2 Nephi.

Nephi refers in the passage just quoted to "the word of the angel of God" as his source for the Messiah's name, and there's reason to think he means the word of the angelic guide from his vision in 1 Nephi. As Joseph Smith originally dictated the text, 1 Nephi 12:18 has the angel speak of "the justice of the Eternal God and Jesus Christ, which is the Lamb of God." Joseph Smith replaced "Jesus Christ" with "the Messiah" when preparing the second (1837) edition of the Book of Mormon, but the first (1830) edition reads "Jesus Christ," as in the manuscript sources. The prophet apparently wondered in 1837 whether the text's reference to "Jesus Christ" was out of place, appearing in advance of the name's actual revelation. But 2 Nephi 25:19 confirms the text's consistency.[5] It seems Nephi learned the Messiah's name soon after leaving Jerusalem, although he largely leaves specificity for the sermons of 2 Nephi. ☞

The specificity of Nephi's prophecies shapes his comments on the Messiah. Because Nephi anticipates the Messiah's (first) coming at a specific but distant point in the future—and at a specific but distant geographical location—the Messiah's coming is at once localized and globalized. It's local in the sense that it can't usher in the end of history. It occurs far away from scattered Israel, when prophecies of gathering remain unfulfilled. It therefore occurs long before what Nephi's angel calls "the end of the world" (1 Ne. 14:22). The Messiah's coming is global too, though. It's global in that it isn't solely about redeeming Israelites in and around Jerusalem. Instead, as Lehi already points out, it's about "the redemption of the world" (1:19). And it concretely introduces the world to the Lamb who

☞ After Jacob's revelation of the name "Christ" in 2 Nephi 10, it appears five times more frequently than "the Messiah." After Nephi's revelation of the name "Jesus Christ" in 2 Nephi 25, it appears nine times more frequently than does "the Messiah."

works throughout history to bring about redemption. Nephi nicely captures this double meaning of his Messiah when he predicts the local crucifixion of "the God of Abraham, and of Isaac, and the God of Jacob" in Jerusalem but then predicts also the global effects of that event, with "the kings of the isles of the sea" exclaiming, "The God of nature suffers" (19:10, 12). The God of Abraham, Isaac, and Jacob, but also the God of nature—such is the essence of Nephi's Messiah.

Another of Nephi's titles for the Messiah captures this same double meaning. Drawing a divine title from the Book of Isaiah (see 1 Ne. 19:23; 20:17; 21:7, 26), Nephi speaks often of "the Redeemer." At times, though, the Redeemer is "the Redeemer of the world" (10:5; 11:27), while at others he's "the Redeemer, the Mighty One of Israel" (22:12). Similarly, it's "the gospel of their Redeemer" that latter-day Lamanites must come to know (15:14), but it's in learning of the gathering of "all . . . the house of Israel" that believers will "remember the Lord their Redeemer" (19:16–18). The redemption of the whole world can't be disentangled from the local redemption of Israel in 1 Nephi. It's "the very God of Israel" who becomes Lamb, Messiah, Jesus Christ, and Redeemer (verse 7).

Yet another name for the Messiah deserves close attention. As Nephi moves from his synopsis of Lehi's sermon in 1 Nephi 10 to the account of his own visionary experience, he speaks of "faith on the Son of God" and then clarifies that "the Son of God" is "the Messiah who should come" (verse 17). All of Nephi's talk about the God of Israel being the Messiah might seem at first to leave little room for teachings about other members of what Latter-day Saints call the Godhead. Where would the Father and the Holy Ghost fit into this picture? But when Nephi calls the Messiah the Son, questions about the Father and the Spirit must be raised.

The way the Godhead is described in the Book of Mormon is confusing for many readers. Abinadi's discussion of how God is "the Father and the Son" is especially difficult (Mosiah 15:2). At first glance, however, Nephi's treatment of the Godhead seems more accessible to us than Abinadi's. When Nephi provides his fullest exposition of the meaning of the Lamb's baptism in 2 Nephi 31, he distinguishes the Father, the Son, and the Holy Ghost pretty straightforwardly. The Son witnesses his obedience to the Father in baptism, and he therefore receives the Holy Ghost from the Father. Here we seem to have three distinct beings, as Joseph Smith taught. But when we turn to 1 Nephi, things seem strikingly less clear. For example, in the abridgment of Lehi's record (1 Nephi 1–9), there's no talk of "the Father" or "the Son." There are many references to "God," "the Lord," and "the Lord God," but are these supposed to refer to the Father or to the Son? Things seem less ambiguous at first in Nephi's own proceedings (1 Nephi 10–22); there readers find many references to "the Father" and "the Son" in what seem to be straightforward passages. Closer reading, however, makes even these less apparently confusing passages seem more difficult.

At first glance, though, 1 Nephi's references to the Father and the Son really do seem simple. If one grabs a current edition of the Book of Mormon and looks at 1 Nephi 11:21 and 1 Nephi 13:40, for example, she'll see that these verses identify "the Lamb of God" as "the Son of the Eternal Father." Doesn't Nephi therefore quite straightforwardly distinguish the Son from the Father? But much earlier editions of the Book of Mormon suggest that there's something strange afoot in these and related passages. In the first (1830) edition, for instance, these passages don't say that "the Lamb of God" is "*the*

56

Son of the Eternal Father"; they say, instead, that he is simply "*the Eternal Father.*" And this is no printer's mistake; the handwritten manuscripts from the Book of Mormon's translation confirm it. Joseph Smith altered the text for the second (1837) edition of the Book of Mormon. He changed two other passages in a similar way. In 1 Nephi 11:32 the prophet added "the Son of" to "the everlasting God" in yet another description of the Lamb, and in 1 Nephi 11:18 he changed a description of the Virgin as "the mother of God" to read "the mother of the Son of God" (see FIGURE 10).[6]

Why would Joseph Smith change these passages? It apparently wasn't because he felt it inappropriate to describe Jesus Christ as the Eternal Father, since other passages in the Book of Mormon call Christ the Father, and the prophet made no changes in those other passages (see Mosiah 3:8; 15:2–4; 16:15; Alma 11:39; 3 Ne. 1:14; Ether 3:14). Latter-day Saints have thus long since found ways of explaining in what ways it's appropriate to speak of Christ as the Father. It's unclear why the changes were introduced, but it's apparent that passages in 1 Nephi that might seem to draw simple distinctions between the Father and the Son are more complicated than they appear. Are there, then, *no* passages in 1 Nephi where the Father and the Son are distinguished as straightforwardly as in 2 Nephi 31? Actually, there's at least one that points in the same direction as the last chapters of 2 Nephi. In 1 Nephi 12:18, the same passage already discussed in which the name "Jesus Christ" originally appeared, we find a relatively clear formula that sounds much like 2 Nephi 31. There, Nephi's angelic guide speaks of "the Eternal God, and Jesus Christ which is the Lamb of God, of whom the Holy Ghost beareth record from the beginning of the world until this time, and from this time henceforth

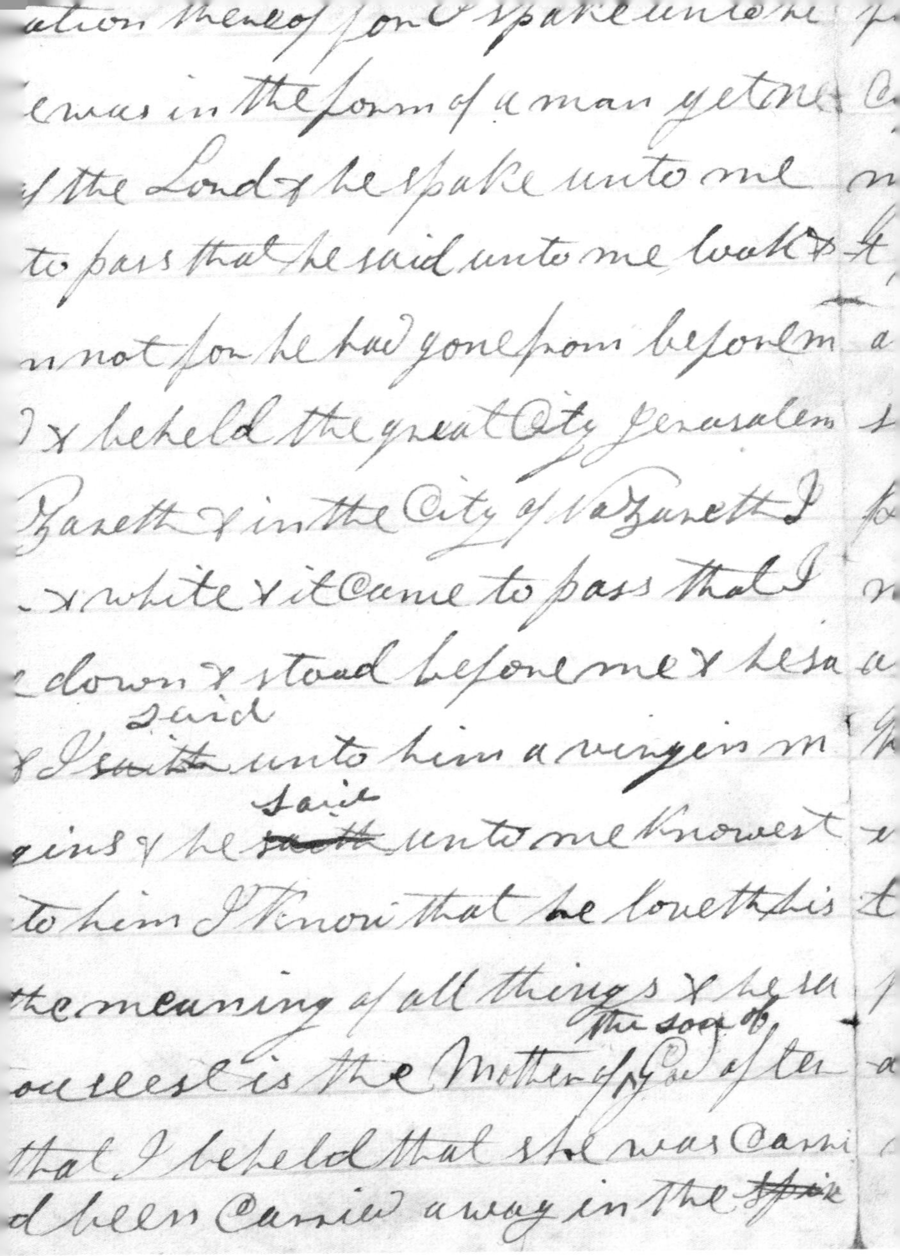

FIGURE 10 Joseph Smith changed a description of the Virgin as "the mother of God" to read "the mother of the Son of God" (1 Nephi 11:18). A close-up image of p. 16 of the printer's manuscript of the Book of Mormon (the lower right-hand corner of the image), as visible in *Joseph Smith Papers Revelations and Translations*, Volume 3, Part 1, p. 50. © Intellectual Reserve, Inc.

and forever." Here the name for the divine being we call "the Father" is apparently "the Eternal God."

It seems, in the end, that God the Father *is* present in 1 Nephi, although he seems content to remain largely in the background, letting the spotlight shine principally on his Son. We might put the same point the following way. It's the Messiah before whom Nephi most wishes to bring his readers in 1 Nephi. As Nephi sees things, the Father works primarily to set the Lamb before the world.

We haven't yet said much about the Holy Spirit. What of the third member of the Godhead? Here, too, we find peculiarities in 1 Nephi, but peculiarities that are less confusing than simply intriguing. The book contains forty-six references to the Spirit, which use a number of different titles ("the Spirit," "the Holy Spirit," "the Spirit of God," "the Spirit of the Lord," and so on). There's something, though, about one title in particular: "the Holy Ghost." This name accounts for nine of the forty-six references to the Spirit, but while the other titles are evenly distributed throughout 1 Nephi, "the Holy Ghost" appears *only* in the original chapter III (1 Ne. 10–14), Nephi's apocalyptic vision. And this is no fluke. 2 Nephi also uses the title "the Holy Ghost" only in Nephi's own prophecies, and only in those that directly refer to or build on the apocalyptic vision in 1 Nephi. Other titles for the Spirit, though, are again evenly distributed throughout 2 Nephi. Nephi apparently sees "the Holy Ghost" as a peculiar title, relevant only in certain contexts. (It's likely no coincidence that it appears only where "the Lamb of God" also serves as the privileged title for Jesus Christ in Nephi's record.)

There are other ways that Nephi's conception of the Spirit is unique. In the Old Testament, God's Spirit is an overpowering force, often heedless of human agency. In the most extreme example of this phenomenon, "the

Spirit of God" came on Saul, and he "prophesied" and "stripped off his clothes also, . . . and lay down naked all that day and all that night" (1 Sam. 19:23–24). The writers of the Old Testament seem to have understood the Spirit as something human beings have no real power to resist. By contrast, when Nephi finds himself "constrained by the Spirit" to do something he dislikes, he finds he can struggle against the divine influence (1 Ne. 4:10). And it's striking that his resistance seems to force the Spirit to *speak*, something the Spirit doesn't do in the Old Testament. Nephi ends up having a conversation with the Spirit, built around arguments and explanations. Sometime later, Nephi finds he again has the ability to speak "as a man speaketh" to the Spirit "in the form of a man" (11:11). ☞ Nephi's relationship to the Spirit repeatedly forces the Spirit to make its nature manifest in peculiar ways. And it's this intriguing and unique relationship to the Spirit that leads Nephi to a visionary experience in which the Spirit appears for the first time under the title "the Holy Ghost." Nephi thus appears to have a unique conception of the Spirit, and he seems to believe that the title "the Holy Ghost" is as apocalyptic as the title "the Lamb of God."

Despite these peculiarities, the principal role of the Holy Ghost in Nephi's record is simple enough. The Holy Ghost unfolds "the mysteries of God" (1 Ne. 10:19) and works in power on those "who shall seek to bring forth [God's] Zion" (13:37). Above all, in the passage that most straightforwardly distinguishes Father, Son, and Spirit, the Holy Ghost "beareth record" of "the Eternal God and Jesus Christ which is the Lamb" (12:18). Just as the Father works principally in 1 Nephi to proffer

☞ Some suggest that "the Spirit of the Lord" here refers to the premortal spirit body of Jesus Christ. While an interesting interpretation, this doesn't account for the fact that all other references to "the Spirit of the Lord" in First Nephi clearly refer to the Holy Spirit (see 1 Ne. 1:12; 7:14, 15; 11:1; 13:15; 15:12).

his Son, the Spirit in Nephi's record assumes the task of testifying of the Messiah. Throughout 1 Nephi, we might say, the whole of the Godhead works conjointly to set the Lamb of God before the world. Israel's God, for Nephi, is first and foremost Jesus Christ, Lamb and Messiah, and the Father through the Holy Ghost works to make this clear to the whole world. Certainly, in the end, it's to a knowledge of *this* God—the Lamb and the Messiah—that Israel must come in the last day, when the promises to Abraham are fulfilled.

Since the early 1980s, the Book of Mormon has been graced with a subtitle: "Another Testament of Jesus Christ." This is wholly appropriate for a book that attributes detailed knowledge of the Messiah's life, ministry, and mission to prophets some six centuries before the birth of Jesus of Nazareth. The gift of prophecy among the Nephites had a unique form, characterized by remarkable "plainness" (2 Ne. 25:4). And so we today find the Book of Mormon a strikingly clear guide to the life we hope to live in Christ. It's true that the book sometimes seems unsure about how best to teach the nature of God the Father, but its teachings about Christ shine a beacon of hope to every struggling human being seeking rest and redemption. This begins already with 1 Nephi, where Christ stands at center stage. From Lehi's talk of the Messiah through the angel's talk of the Lamb to Nephi's talk of the Redeemer, Christ is the hero of the covenantal story Nephi has to tell.

But Nephi never lets us forget that Christ's work is the work of fulfilling the promises given anciently to Abraham. He speaks of those who, in the last days, will "come to the knowledge of their Redeemer and the very points of his doctrine, that they may know how to come unto him and be saved." But in the same breath, he explains that these are "the remnant" of Israel and that they also must "know that they are of the house of Israel, and that they are the covenant people of the Lord"; they must "know and come to the knowledge of their forefathers" (1 Ne. 15:14). To know Christ is to know the covenant, for Nephi. And it follows that to know the covenant is to know Christ, to begin to appreciate what Christ makes possible for the whole world. The Restoration is about Christ *and* the covenant, in the end, and it's Nephi who makes that clearest—until Jesus Christ himself appears among Lehi's children to confirm everything Nephi has said. From 1 Nephi to 3 Nephi, the message is the same. The Lamb works to redeem us by bringing us all together as one covenant people.

PART II

The Theological
Questions of 1 Nephi

4

Laban's Death

A dark Jerusalem street, a drunken man unconscious on the ground, a youth holding a sword over the helpless man's head—the scene looks more suspicious than heroic. And then you run into that youth sometime later and demand an explanation. His answer? "God told me to do it." Could that possibly be satisfactory? "Did you hesitate at all?" "Some, yes, but God made clear what I was to do." How could you trust someone who feels so confident about paradoxical commands? . . .

the problem

Questions about the Book of Mormon's truth tend to be of two sorts. First, we want to know whether it all really happened. Second, we want to know whether it really shows us who God is. These questions, though, don't weigh the same for all readers.

First, then, we might ask whether the book is true *to history*. Was there a real Nephi who lived anciently and wrote these things? This question arises when we encounter arguments that the book came out of Joseph Smith's head rather than the ancient world. Books and articles that contain such arguments, along with books and articles defending the book's antiquity, are abundant—a testament to our worries, and to our confidence that there are reasons to be reassured. It's worth noting, though, that this first sort of question doesn't keep all (maybe not even most) readers up at night. They trust that their spiritual convictions settle the question or that others can and will do the work of intellectually defending the Book of Mormon's ancientness.

But a second sort of question about the book's truth can steal along and worry any reader. This time the question is whether the book is true *to God*. Granted there was a Nephi who lived anciently and wrote these things, *can we trust him* in things of the Spirit? Are we sure he's a reliable witness for God? Prophets aren't infallible, and so it wouldn't be surprising if Nephi gets something wrong now and again. Could he get something so seriously wrong that he leads us astray? We seldom voice these worries so bluntly, but there's a considerable literature here too. For instance, it's easy to find expressions of concern about the lack of female voices in the Book of Mormon—a problem already in 1 Nephi. Some conclude that the book is the inadvertent victim of near-universal misogyny in the ancient world, but that very fact might well leave us wondering whether to trust scriptural authors who don't defend or promote the equality of the sexes. In a similar vein, it's increasingly easy to find critiques of how Nephi presents Laman and Lemuel. We're apt to feel that Nephi is unfair to his understandably baffled brothers and that maybe they were right to see Nephi as self-righteous and judgmental. If so, shouldn't we worry that Nephi lacks common feeling, that he was spiritually gifted but socially clueless? And could someone like that really be a reliable guide to living a rich spiritual life in community with others?

We'll return to these concerns in chapters 5 and 6. First, though, we'll look at another reason people worry about whether to trust Nephi as a spiritual figure. This is the killing of Laban.[1] Some readers aren't bothered by the story, but most find it troubling. The sheer volume of what's been written to explain or justify Nephi's actions betrays our collective discomfort with the event.

The literature on this matter outweighs the literature on Laman and Lemuel and on 1 Nephi's women several times over. This story makes us wonder how we should feel about the Book of Mormon as scripture. Should we trust Nephi's God if he commands believers to kill defenseless people, however wicked they might be? Should we trust Nephi if he believes God would command such a thing? It's not only true that "this passage from the Book of Mormon is used by anti-Mormons to attack the book and by investigators to reject it." It's true also that "some Mormons themselves . . . use the passage to justify troubling, violent rhetoric and even violent action."[2] Sorting out the meaning of Laban's slaying may literally be a matter of life and death. How do we make sense of the story?

The main difficulty is that Nephi's God seems too ready to assign him a violent task. We tend to feel that sheer necessity would justify execution. That is, if there were no other way to get Nephi out of Jerusalem with the brass plates, we could feel that Nephi's God was just in commanding Nephi to kill Laban. But it doesn't require much imagination to think of ways God might have made escape possible without such drastic measures. It's the unnecessary nature of the gruesome violence that bothers us. Why not solve the problem another way? Why would God command such an unnecessary thing and Nephi record it?

It isn't enough just to identify the problem, however, and we mustn't draw critical conclusions too quickly. We want real solutions, solutions yielded only in full honesty about the difficulty of the text. How can we begin to work toward a good theological reading of the text?

Might understanding come from the Spirit's words to Nephi on the occasion? The Spirit seems to offer three nested explanations for the killing, but none of them provides clear comfort. The first—God has delivered Laban into Nephi's hands (see 1 Ne. 4:11, 12)—makes subtle allusion to Exodus 21:13, a snippet of scripture that might suggest that the killing would be "an excusable homicide under the public law" of the time.[3] But this satisfies only if we assume that what's legal is moral, a questionable assumption. The second explanation—"The Lord slayeth the wicked to bring forth his righteous purposes" (1 Ne. 4:13)—builds on the first and reserves to God alone any decision about when "righteous purposes" require untimely death. This is perhaps encouraging, but this explanation offers no rational justification, making God's actions a mystery. Hence the Spirit's final and most famous explanation: "It is better that one man should perish than that a nation should dwindle and perish in unbelief" (verse 13). This seems meant to explain God's purposes by speaking of a nation that needs saving. But because it replaces all talk of God with an abstract moral calculus, it's probably the most disconcerting of the Spirit's words. Numbers games work only theoretically; at the practical level, they question the real value of individual lives. It isn't surprising that a principle like this has been used to justify wicked violence, violence presented as necessary for the fulfillment of God's righteous purposes.

Might understanding come instead, then, from Nephi's reflections in response to the Spirit's words? Nephi certainly specifies what God's "righteous purposes" are. After the Spirit's explanations, Nephi says, "I knew that the Lord had delivered Laban into my hands for this cause—that I might obtain the records according to his commandments" (verse 17). Given the brass plates' importance for Nephi's project, this makes some sense. The text "underscores the monumental—yes, even life-and-death—importance of sacred scripture."[4]

The whole Lehite nation about to arise might have gone without what was "engraven upon the plates of brass" (verse 16). And Nephi knew that "they could not keep the commandments of the Lord according to the law of Moses, save they should have the law" (verse 15). Here, indeed, are righteous purposes, and perhaps purposes important enough to justify God arranging for the death of a wicked man. But not everyone will feel comfortable with this way of settling affairs. One scholar suggests, "While there is no question that the possession of the plates was important to Nephi and his people, we must be careful not to ignore the unlimited alternative ways to acquire the plates without Nephi having to kill Laban."[5] Mustn't there be another explanation, a better or more satisfying one?

potential solutions

Many have offered further explanations. Perhaps best known among scholarly explanations is the legal one already mentioned.[6] Although it might help to distance Nephi's action from murder, this approach (as we've already noted) fails to distinguish between legal and ethical justification. Even if Nephi's actions were technically legal, it isn't obvious that we should be comforted by the fact. Much was legally permissible under the Law of Moses about which we'd have moral qualms today (slavery, to take a simple example). Ethical questions generally eclipse legal questions for good reason. It's a mistake to ignore the ethical in any serious analysis of Laban's death. But then interpreters who focus on ethics face their own temptation. In an increasingly secularized world, there's heavy pressure to take strictly rational ethical demands as absolute. This has its own costs, among them a growing cultural assumption that religion should be rejected because it occasionally questions or claims to supersede public reason. Within such a worldview, it's easy to decide in advance that there's no moral justification for Nephi's killing of Laban, and so it remains only to show how Nephi's violent action betrays his entrapment in a mythical, unenlightened worldview—one that excludes the full revelation of Jesus Christ (who embodies rational ethics).

More theologically interesting, therefore, are readings of the Laban episode that recognize how the religious exceeds the ethical (in something like the way the ethical exceeds the legal). Such readings tend to speak of "an Abrahamic test."[7] Radical obedience or faith demands a sacrifice not only of objects or possessions one holds dear but also and especially of certain *attitudes* or *worldviews*. Real faith—faith in its richest form—therefore demonstrates itself in situations where obedience looks like suspension of the ethical attitudes one shares with everyone else.[8] Abraham's offering of Isaac might be such a thing. Abraham's action looks to outsiders like either vicious murder or tragic sacrifice, but what Abraham does on Moriah is obedience, beyond the immorality of murder and the morality of sacrifice. And this makes Abraham's actions incomprehensible. Nephi's actions might be approached similarly. God demands of Nephi something shocking to our ethical sensibilities—sensibilities Nephi shares (see 1 Ne. 4:10)—because it might help him and us to smash the rational and ethical idols we're tempted to place before the God of faith and obedience.

Such a reading recognizes the right place of ethics in any theologically satisfying account of faith. That is, it recognizes that religion claims priority for God over human intellectual constructions, even those we feel deeply. It certainly feels perverse to demand that God prove his ethical bona fides to us, even and especially if we trust that our own sense of right and wrong is a gift from God. But despite its theological appeal in a certain regard, even this approach to Laban's killing is ultimately unsatisfying. Obviously, it would be distasteful to secular individuals who worry about religion overstepping the limits of reason. But it's unsatisfying also and especially to believers because it fails to take seriously the actual text of 1 Nephi. It imposes a theological frame on the text without asking how Nephi tells the story of his encounter with Laban. What's needed prior to a genuinely convincing theological account of Laban's death is a solid reading of the story in which it appears.

Of course, scholars have analyzed interesting literary elements in the story. Some consider how Nephi's story echoes biblical narratives that might explain the political substance of the story. Others consider aspects of the narrative framing of the event and how these affect readers' expectations. Still others consider how the text repeats certain words and ideas, helping to focus the narrative.[9] We must go further, however. It's essential to recognize how 1 Nephi's structure guides reading and then to read more carefully the conversation between Nephi and the Spirit at the climax of the story. In other words, we have to read the slaying of Laban as an integral part of the original chapter I, not as a standalone story. And we'll see that what's central to the larger story of what's now 1 Nephi 1–5 is a story about the word *commandments*.

The original chapter I opens with Lehi's visions in Jerusalem, and these quickly result in his family's removal from the city. Once the group sets up camp near the Red Sea, Nephi introduces readers to the actual members of the family. First we meet Laman and Lemuel, described as murmuring and potentially murderous (see 1 Ne. 2:11–13). Nephi then introduces himself as "young," "large," and eager "to know the

72

mysteries of God" (verse 16). To understand Lehi's actions, Nephi cries to God, has his heart softened, and talks to his brothers about his experience. Sam, we're told, "believed" (verse 17), but Laman and Lemuel don't "hearken" (verse 18). This drives Nephi to pray again, and he hears a divine voice. And it's what this voice says that really gets the story off the ground.

In this first divine communication, God twice draws Nephi's attention to keeping commandments. First, Nephi hears this: "And inasmuch as ye shall keep my commandments, ye shall prosper, and shall be led to a land of promise" (verse 20). This oft-repeated promise parallels a second: "And inasmuch as thou shalt keep my commandments, thou shalt be made a ruler and a teacher over thy brethren" (verse 22). Both verses focus on keeping commandments, but each makes a different promise: the one about prosperity in a promised land, the other about rule and ministry. There's a subtler difference between the two verses, though: Each uses a distinct pronoun. The first promise uses "ye," the second "thou." The Book of Mormon isn't always consistent on fine grammatical points, but "ye" is technically plural, while "thou" is technically singular. The promise about prosperity in the promised land thus seems to concern the whole family, while the promise about ruling and teaching is apparently for Nephi alone. This makes sense. Nephi's faithfulness would determine his role in the new colony, but the whole colony's faithfulness would determine their collective prosperity.

The two promises made through Nephi in 1 Nephi 2 are key to the larger narrative, as any reader of the Book of Mormon knows. Both promises, moreover, concern "commandments." This word, it turns out, is the linchpin for the story that follows.

Immediately after hearing promises to those who keep commandments, Nephi returns to his father and hears about a commandment. Lehi has "dreamed a dream" and must send his sons to Jerusalem for the brass plates (1 Ne. 3:2). In commissioning Nephi, Lehi refers to commandments exactly three times, as if to signal their divine source (see verses 2, 4, 5). When Nephi famously responds ("I will go and do"), he *also* refers to commandments exactly three times, apparently confirming that he's understood the message (verse 7). And he certainly has understood the message. Nephi has just heard directly from God that everything he hopes for depends on keeping commandments, and now his father gives him a clear commandment from God. Nephi understands, and he expresses his youthful zeal in pursuing the fulfillment of God's promises.

Lehi's commission, however, may unintentionally constrict Nephi's understanding of God's promises. Lehi introduces the task but then reports that Nephi's brothers murmur, "saying it is a hard thing which I have required of them" (verse 5). He also promises Nephi he will be "favored of the Lord" for not murmuring (verse 6). Such talk would fill the head of even a faithful youth (and maybe *especially* a faithful youth) with visions of grandeur. If Nephi keeps this commandment—which has come so soon after he's heard from God—he, the youngest, will be ruler and teacher over his older brothers. Lehi's words inadvertently help to narrow Nephi's focus from the whole group's responsibility to keep commandments to just his own. What began as two distinct promises becomes just one. It seems Nephi, writing long after the events recounted, wishes readers to see how the promise given specifically to him quickly came in his young mind to obscure the promise given through him to the whole family.

The story that follows amply demonstrates Nephi's ambition. It falls to Laman to make the first attempt to retrieve the plates when the boys arrive in Jerusalem. When that goes badly, Nephi suddenly emerges as the force that keeps things moving, first through a daring speech. Interestingly, although his speech alludes to a new plan, Nephi doesn't actually explain the plan in the speech as it's recorded in the text. He mentions that Lehi "left gold and silver, and all manner of riches" when leaving Jerusalem (verse 16), but he doesn't explain what he intends to do with that wealth. Instead, he presents himself as having become distracted by the fact that Lehi faithfully left his wealth behind "because of the commandments of the Lord" (verse 16). It seems that this is what's really central to Nephi's zealous speech: keeping commandments. Four times in the short speech he mentions commandments, and the summary verse that follows the speech mentions them once more.

The speech thus accomplishes one thing rather than another. It reveals not Nephi's plan for moving forward but rather just the fact that Nephi is acutely anxious about keeping commandments. It also shows that he's willing to impose this anxiety on his brothers. And, actually, the speech does one other thing too. It provides Nephi with his first opportunity to explain what he assumes God's purposes are with the plates: to "preserve unto our children the language of our fathers" and to "preserve unto them the words . . . of all the holy prophets" (verses 19–20). These are noble notions, and they may be right in crucial ways. But it's unclear how Nephi could have known them at the time. In commissioning Nephi, Lehi has spoken only of the plates containing "the record of the Jews and also a genealogy" (verse 3). And as we'll see, Nephi will learn forcefully that he hasn't fully understood God's intentions. He's making good guesses, but he also seems to speak too soon and to be too sure of himself.

It seems, then, that Nephi tells the story so as to make readers wonder whether he was ready for what God promised him. Was he interested in keeping commandments, or did he treat the commandments primarily as something to force himself into his role as ruler and teacher? His first efforts at teaching seem distracted and anxious, built on (educated) guesses. As for his leadership skills, Nephi's first plan to retrieve the plates fails as spectacularly as Laman's. And it's striking that we learn nothing of Nephi's mental state after this failure. Is he depressed, aware that he has perhaps overreached? Or is he as confident as ever? We don't know. Instead, we're directed to Laman and Lemuel's fury as they famously beat him and Sam. We're quite sure about the oldest brothers' mental state, but Nephi leaves his readers wondering about what his preliminary failures in teaching and ruling mean for him.

Then an angel appears. Nephi receives physical deliverance, and perhaps he receives psychological deliverance too. The angel asks an important rhetorical question of Laman and Lemuel: "Know ye not that the Lord hath chosen [Nephi] to be a ruler over you, and this because of your iniquities?" (1 Ne. 3:29). Even if Nephi has overreached, he's still "chosen," and now his brothers know it. Unsurprisingly, then, Nephi attempts a second speech after the angel withdraws. This second speech is sharper, more direct, and more consistent than the first. This time Nephi makes no oaths, uses more rhetorically forceful illustrations, and genuinely encourages faith. He seems to have shed his anxiety as well, referring to commandments just once and apparently in response to his brothers' ironic complaint that Laban (rather than the Lord) "can command fifty" (verse 31). Nephi thus appears to portray himself as having changed his outlook after the angel's visit. Certainly, his final attempt to retrieve the plates begins on a new note: "And I was led by the Spirit, not knowing beforehand the things which I should do" (4:6). It seems Nephi is done making educated guesses and plans of his own. He's ready to follow the Spirit.

It's precisely "the Spirit," however, that Nephi has to confront in Jerusalem. Nephi finds Laban in the dark city, but he's drunk and incapacitated. The Spirit proves livelier and perhaps more dangerous.

With Laban's sword already in his hand, Nephi is "constrained by the Spirit" to "kill Laban" (1 Ne. 4:10). In light of all that's come before this point in the story, Nephi's word choice here is striking. He speaks of the Spirit's *constraint*, not of the Spirit's *commandment*. Are we meant to notice the change in terminology? Are we to understand that Nephi is confronted with something different at this point, something he's free to resist or right to question? Or does Nephi hope to distract us from the fact that his "hesitancy is in direct contrast to his earlier bold proclamation" of zeal?[10] It's a symptomatic moment, rich with meaning and ambiguity. It's apparent, though, that Nephi's faith is unsure. The angel has confirmed his chosenness, but then Nephi shrinks and resists the Spirit into whose care he's supposedly put himself. All this means that when the Spirit goes on to explain things, Nephi's reflections aren't exercises in abstract reasoning. He's at a spiritual crossroads, in the midst of an existential crisis.

This is most important to remember at the climax of the Spirit's communication. When Nephi hears the Spirit say, "It is better that one man should perish than that a nation should dwindle and perish in unbelief" (1 Ne. 4:13), the words have a very specific effect on him. Nephi never defends the idea of an abstract moral calculus. He says instead that the Spirit's statement reminded him of something he'd forgotten—something we as readers have watched him forget. "And now, when I, Nephi, had heard these words," he says, "I remembered the words of the Lord which he spake unto me in the wilderness, saying that: Inasmuch as *thy seed* shall keep my commandments, they shall prosper in the land of promise" (verse 14; italics added). What Nephi has forgotten and has to remember is the first promise God made to him, a promise concerned with his whole family and not just himself and his own grandiose future. When he hears the Spirit speak of "a nation," Nephi apparently sees for the first time his own (potentially) selfish motivations for keeping commandments. He's prioritized his own promises over those of everyone else. God apparently prioritizes the promises to all.

It's this realization in the story that convinces Nephi to "obey the voice of the Spirit" (4:18). It isn't enough that the Lord delivers Laban into his hands. It isn't enough that Laban has flouted God's commandments. It's when Nephi sees God's covenantal promises to whole peoples that he sees how his own strivings for covenantal righteousness are tainted with a competitive spirit. This gets him over his own sense of self-righteousness, bringing him to climactic obedience. We might say also that he realizes he's misunderstood the meaning of the word *commandments* in God's promises to him and Lehi's children more generally. It doesn't refer to whatever God happens to instruct one to do, as Nephi's actions would suggest he assumed at first. It refers rather to "the commandments of the Lord according to the law of Moses," words needed for the benefit of a whole people (verse 15). The brass plates contain the law that will guide Lehi's children in the promised land.

However one makes sense of the Spirit's constraint, we must read the text within the story of Nephi's maturing faith and relationship to God. This is how Nephi tells the story. And what he sees as most crucial, according to the logic of his story, is how he came to see that his relationship to God had been wrongly bound up with his ego. Only once he'd seen this problem could he begin to worry rightly about how God might work through him for the good of a whole nation. Of course, we haven't yet done enough to show that this is the right way to read 1 Nephi. And many would be inclined to say that Nephi's experience with Laban doesn't seem to have shaken Nephi's self-confidence much at all. He still seems quite sure of himself in the remainder of his story. It turns out, though, that there's a larger pattern in 1 Nephi—admittedly subtle but no less real for that—of Nephi noting how his zeal often overreached his grasp of what God was doing with and through him. Other instances of this pattern will draw our attention in the next chapter.

What are we supposed to learn from the Laban episode? Nephi tells us what he learned from it: that his youthful zeal was more self-serving than focused on God or other human beings. Might we come to see the same thing in ourselves? Don't we balk at the Spirit's constraint for reasons similar to Nephi's? We're so often driven by self-centered desires to be rulers and teachers in our own rights. For some, this takes the shape of looking down on those who supposedly aren't obedient or righteous enough—perhaps because they do things like raise questions about whether Nephi was right to take Laban's life. For others, this takes the shape of self-congratulating intellectual superiority, criticizing supposedly naive believers—perhaps because they aren't properly scandalized by a story like that of Laban's slaying. But maybe in too quickly accepting *or* too quickly rejecting Nephi's actions we fail to get the point of Nephi's story. Isn't the point that it's hard to be critical without being hypocritical? How can we see the mote in another's eye without casting the beam from our own?

There are motes in Nephi's eyes, to be sure—maybe even beams. But what's remarkable about the way Nephi tells his story is that he seems to hope we'll see those motes, or even those beams. And most likely we're supposed to see ourselves in the story, mote- or beam-ridden eyes and all. Nephi learned through his encounter with the Spirit that God's purposes are bigger than our own. The communal and the covenantal are to be privileged above our individual—and often selfish—concerns. We're proud of our modern individualism, but Nephi's story suggests there's something important beyond our cloistered concerns. We're not to be hermits, demonstrating our individual righteousness to God and others in our withdrawal from the world. We're meant to live together in love, jointly keeping the commandments and making wherever we live a land of promise.

5

Laman and Lemuel

Perhaps you once pictured Nephi writing in his journal, "Well, my brothers are still idiots. How long do I have to be patient with them before I'm allowed to pummel them?" Perhaps Laman and Lemuel didn't just seem wicked. They seemed stupidly wicked, as if they couldn't see what was right in front of their faces. How hard is it to trust a little more or to learn from miracles? When we're the youthful Nephi's age, the world seems black and white. Closer to Laman's or Lemuel's age, things seem more complicated . . .

family trouble

Ongoing family conflict makes 1 Nephi a sober book. It's also, however, the source for the book's action and intrigue. Visions and sermons occasionally interrupt the struggle among Lehi's sons, but it's never long before everyone is fighting again. In all the stories of conflict, it seems obvious that Nephi is the hero and Laman and Lemuel the villains. Laman and Lemuel seem always in the wrong, Nephi always in the right. Nephi never apologizes (and never needs to, it appears); it's always Laman and Lemuel who must "bow down" and ask for forgiveness (1 Ne. 7:20). And so, by far the most common approach to 1 Nephi has been to treat it as a series of illustrations of faithfulness amid adversity. This is unsurprising in a religious culture focused on the practicalities of family life. Such a reading makes for enjoyably dramatic scriptural storytelling, with lessons that are obvious and memorable.

The very obviousness of the lessons, however, undercuts their force somewhat. Scholars have long noted a "tendency to see Nephi, like Joseph [in Genesis], as a favored son who somewhat insensitively and self-righteously intrudes upon his brothers' feelings."[1] And this tendency won't disappear any time soon. Nephi's obedience can seem so extreme that readers can't identify with him. It's easier to identify with his brothers—with Laman, the relapsing sinner; Lemuel, the follower bowing to social pressure; or Sam, the quiet believer. Among these more human figures, Nephi looks almost pathologically faithful. He certainly appears superhuman, displaying obedience that readers feel they can't themselves muster. It's inevitable that some readers will wonder whether Nephi's obedience is more a liability than an asset. He doesn't show much compassion for his brothers' struggles to believe, and so 1 Nephi can feel blunt and artless, lacking the textured complexity of Old Testament narrative.

Is Nephi's portrayal of Laman and Lemuel fair? Were they as wicked as the text suggests? In a passage worth quoting at length, one scholar defends them using clues from Nephi's own narrative:

> Whatever else they may have been, Laman and Lemuel appear to have been orthodox, observant Jews. Nephi—who has a vested interest in revealing their moral shortcomings—never accuses them of idolatry, false swearing, Sabbath breaking, drunkenness, adultery, or ritual uncleanness. Indeed, when he is describing their sins during their voyage to the New World that bring upon them the wrath of God, the worst he can come up with is "rudeness." . . . It is true that Nephi several times describes Laman and Lemuel as would-be murderers,

but they seem to be rather halfhearted assassins. Although there are two of them, both living side by side with Nephi for years on end, they never kill him or even wound him, despite numerous opportunities and provocations. . . . One of the most remarkable observations concerning Laman and Lemuel is that despite their doubts, complaints, and anger, they nevertheless continue to stay with the family. In fact, they usually end up doing exactly what Lehi and Nephi have requested of them.[2]

One can thus make a case that Nephi's portrayal of his brothers reveals its own problematic biases. Nephi may want his brothers to look worse than they really were.

Let's grant for a moment that this is true, that Nephi unfairly represents his brothers. Naturally, certain ethical questions arise. How should we think about a prophet who deliberately portrays his own brothers in a misleading fashion? Some have tried to answer this question, developing an approach to 1 Nephi that's more academically sophisticated than the usual one. Lehi's sons are the ancestors of whole peoples; they aren't just individuals in their own right. Thus, the stories in 1 Nephi might be largely intended to explain the meaning of and motivations for conflicts between the Nephites and their enemies later in the Book of Mormon. (Biblical scholars have long pointed out that something similar happens in the stories making up Genesis.) In fact, we've seen that Nephi produced the small plates decades after the events described there, at a time when "wars and contentions" between Nephites and Lamanites were happening (2 Ne. 5:34). It seems nearly inevitable that 1 Nephi would have a political dimension.[3] We learn later in the Book of Mormon, moreover, that there was a competing Lamanite view of Nephite origins (see Mosiah 10:12–17), and 1 Nephi might have been meant to work against this competing narrative.

It's therefore possible to explain 1 Nephi's one-sidedness as an aspect of national propaganda. The book's purpose might have been partially to convince the Nephites that they were right to resist the Lamanites in battle. Sadly, if this is true, the unfolding story of Nephite-Lamanite relations in the Book of Mormon suggests that the propaganda worked too well. The Nephites were quite ready to despise the Lamanites, generally failing to see "that which was good among them" (Mosiah 9:1). Shortly after Nephi's death, Jacob already had to command the Nephites in God's name to "revile no more against" the Lamanites, whom they'd come to hate "because of the darkness of their skins" (Jacob 3:9). Nephi's own comments regarding his Lamanite enemies' skin color would unfortunately seem to have laid the foundations for these attitudes (see 2 Ne. 5:21–25).

If the political dimension of 1 Nephi helped to create this kind of atmosphere, it's a reason to lament. It might help to explain things, but it's not good news. We'd have some additional historical context, but would this assuage our concerns about Nephi's portrayal of his brothers? How do we come to terms—if at all—with what seems to be Nephi's injustice toward his closest kin?

But perhaps we're too quick to grant that Nephi is unfair to his brothers. What does his total portrait of them look like? Is it significant that 1 Nephi ends on a note of real hope for Laman and Lemuel (despite what then happens in 2 Nephi)? There's reason to think so, as we'll see. Further, we might ask if we're right to feel that Nephi paints an always-rosy picture of himself.

We've seen already that Nephi tells the story of slaying Laban "without concern for preserving a perfect image of himself."[4] Does Nephi want his readers—of whom he's strikingly aware as a writer—to think that he's an example of unswerving obedience? There's reason to doubt this, as we'll see. To proceed, then, we must reconsider 1 Nephi's portraits of both its supposed hero and its apparent villains. And, all things considered, it's probably best to begin with Nephi, whose self-portrayal seems so obviously positive, if not, in fact, self-serving. We can then turn to Laman and Lemuel.

portrait of a protagonist

Nephi comes into his own story only after he presents his oldest brothers and their "stiffneckedness" (1 Ne. 2:11). By contrast with them, Nephi appears submissive and obedient, not at all "like unto the Jews who were at Jerusalem" (verse 13). He's "exceedingly young" but has "great desires to know of the mysteries of God" (verse 16). All of this naturally gives the impression of a young man of faith, ready to follow his father at his word. But Nephi is subtle. He doesn't say that his precocious hunger for divine mystery led him to believe his father—but rather that it led him to ask God for understanding regarding his father's words and actions. The implication is that the young Nephi had doubts and concerns about Lehi, real questions rather than blind obedience. Only because his prayer yielded some kind of "visit" from God did he "not rebel" against Lehi like his brothers. God, he says, "did soften my heart," which implies that his heart was originally, in some sense, hard. Only thanks to God's graceful intervention did he "believe" (verse 16).

Nephi apparently doesn't want us to see him as naturally obedient. He was naturally inquisitive and genuinely open to answers, but this is a different thing.

It's this, though, that really distinguishes Nephi from his brothers. Later, as if to illustrate this specific difference, Nephi goes to God for understanding when he has questions about Lehi's dream, but Laman and Lemuel don't because, as they say, "the Lord maketh no such thing known unto [them]" (1 Ne. 15:9). What's peculiar about Nephi from the beginning is his "great desires to know of the mysteries of God" (2:16). Because he's willing to ask, God gives him to understand. Thus, when Nephi speaks of his brothers' hard hearts, he seems to mean only that they don't believe they can ask and receive. The initial difference between Nephi and his brothers is real, but it's not as great as we tend to assume. And we'll see that even this first illustration of their difference is more complicated than it appears.

We've already reviewed the story of retrieving the brass plates from Laban. We've seen in that story that Nephi doesn't describe his perfect and unerring faith. He implies, rather, that he was too keen to privilege promises made to him over those made to his brothers. He suggests that he tried too hard and too early to assume the role he'd been promised to receive in good time. He describes having invented theological explanations for God's commandments, taking momentous guesses rather than waiting patiently for real understanding. He tells of how his own first attempt to obtain the plates was disastrous, more dangerous and dramatically more expensive than Laman's failed attempt. And he tells how he resisted the Spirit's constraint when what was required was total dependence on God. Nephi repeatedly invites us to see his faith as having needed maturation. Even his celebrated declaration of determined obedience ("I will go and do") may be an expression more of self-centered and youthful zeal than of generous and mature faith.

Nephi, in fact, later seems to revise his original statement of zealous obedience. Early on, he proclaims his knowledge that "the Lord giveth no commandments unto the children of men, save he shall prepare a way for them that they may accomplish the thing which he commandeth them" (1 Ne. 3:7). These words insist that God has a way prepared before giving commandment. After eight years in the desert, though, Nephi speaks differently: "And if it so be that the children of men keep the commandments of God he doth nourish them, and strengthen them, and provide means whereby they can accomplish the thing which he has commanded them" (17:3). Here Nephi says not that God prepares ways and means before giving commandment but rather that he provides ways and means in response to faith and obedience. This is a more realistic—a more mature—perspective on faith. Nephi presumably intends his readers to recognize the shift in perspective as the story develops. Real trust in God seldom looks like self-assured confidence that one can guess at his "wisdom" (3:19). Instead, it most often looks like "not knowing beforehand" what is to be done and how (4:6).

The whole experience of retrieving the plates from Laban must have left Nephi with difficult questions. He knew his brothers' skepticism. Had he pushed them too hard? Had his haste to become a ruler and a teacher alienated them unnecessarily? Could he have secured the plates without a narrow escape, a beating from his brothers, an angelic intervention, and the need to shed blood? There's actually real evidence that Nephi had regrets about how the trip to Jerusalem went.[5] For example, Nephi later inserts into his record a long poem—sometimes called "Nephi's psalm"—that captures his frustrations with himself over his relationship to his brothers (see 2 Ne. 4:15–35).

Tellingly, Nephi notes just before the poem begins that Laman and Lemuel "were angry" with him (4:13). Right after the poem ends, he does this again, generalizing the conflict: "Behold, it came to pass that I, Nephi, did cry much unto the Lord my God, because of the anger of my brethren" (5:1). These bookends suggest that the whole poem is about fraternal conflict. As for the poem itself, it laments not the anger of Nephi's brothers toward him but his anger toward them. He speaks of being "encompassed about" by "temptations" and "sins" (4:18) and admits that he sometimes "give[s] way" (verse 27). But the only temptation or sin specified in the poem is anger. "Why am I angry because of mine enemy?" Nephi asks (verse 27), and he commands himself, "Do not anger again because of mine enemies" (verse 29). The enemies in question must be Laman and Lemuel. Nephi says God "hath confounded" his enemies, "unto the causing of them to quake" (verse 22)—a reference to when he "confounded" Laman and Lemuel in Bountiful, reaching out to "shake" them with God's power (17:52, 54). When Nephi's emotions are visible, he worries more about whether he's mistreated his brothers than about whether they've mistreated him.

Returning to the story of Nephi's maturing faith, we see it continue with a second return to Jerusalem, this time for Ishmael's family. Headed back into the desert, there's a rebellion within the group, involving Laman and Lemuel and also some of Ishmael's family. Nephi rebukes the rebels, and this leads to him being tied up and left "to be devoured by wild beasts" (1 Ne. 7:16). In this precarious situation, Nephi tells us, he offered an interesting prayer for deliverance. "O Lord," he pled, "give me strength that I may burst these bands with which I am bound" (verse 17). Nephi asked for superhuman strength, something spectacular to overawe his brothers. What Nephi says actually happened in response to his prayer is telling, though: "When I had said these words, behold, the bands were loosed from off my hands and feet" (verse 18). This is no small blessing, of course. Nephi was delivered. But his prayer wasn't answered as he hoped. He wished to burst his bands spectacularly, but his bonds were simply loosened. ☞ Nephi apparently wants his readers to see that God delivers on his own divine terms, not with an eye to our (or really, Nephi's) romantic imaginations.

There's more. Nephi predicates his prayer's fulfillment on his faith. In all printed editions of the Book of Mormon, Nephi's prayer includes the words "according to my faith which is in thee" (verse 17), but the original manuscript reads, "according to my faith which is in *me*." Might the original reading suggest that Nephi wished his readers to see his prayer for deliverance as romantically imaginative *and* as too focused on his own role in faith? This is obviously more speculative,[6] but the possibility is real.

At any rate, Nephi's next recorded encounter with his brothers comes after the vision of 1 Nephi 10–14. In 1 Nephi 15, he has an opportunity to explain to Laman and Lemuel the meaning of Lehi's dream. The conversation begins when they say they can't "understand" Lehi's words (verse 7). We've seen that when Nephi asks whether they've petitioned God for understanding, they explain that "the Lord maketh no such thing known unto us" (verse 9). Nephi's response is harsh: "How is it that ye do not keep the commandments of the Lord? How is it that ye will perish, because of the hardness of your hearts?" (verse 10). Nephi's pointed questions may be valid, even if they seem tactless (as Lehi

☞ The passive construction ("were loosed") leaves the agent of the action unclear. It's of course possible (and perhaps most likely) that God is the actor, but Nephi leaves open other possibilities—that, so much more mundanely, one of his defenders comes to his aid or even that Laman or Lemuel feels remorse and loosens his bands.

points out later; see 2 Ne. 1:26). But again one finds that Nephi later suggests he's been too quick to criticize. When his own people, separated from the Lamanites, similarly fail to receive "the spirit of prophecy," Nephi upbraids them more gently and then offers to share his own prophecies with them (2 Ne. 25:4). Here again, Nephi displays the gradual maturation of his faith. His later forms of ruling and teaching retroactively clarify the ways his earlier forms of ruling and teaching needed development. He seems to learn after the fact that it might have been God's will—rather than his brothers' stubbornness—that prevented their reception of a vision.

The pattern is clear. Nephi repeatedly presents his young self as having moved too quickly, overstepped his bounds, or exhibited zeal without full knowledge. It's never obvious at first that this is what's going on. It *becomes* apparent only when Nephi later corrects himself, qualifies his earlier statements, or modifies his earlier zeal. Sometimes clarification comes within a few verses, but it often comes only after dozens of chapters. Nephi's self-critique is thus subtle, but he never hides his story of maturation. He intentionally warns his readers that he's a complex hero—a protagonist, to be sure, but an imperfect one. And so, if we see Nephi as exemplarily obedient and infallible from the beginning or, alternatively, as rigidly inflexible and overbearing throughout, we've missed the point. As Nephi tells the story, he's more like a "huge, rough stone rolling down from a high mountain," smoothed out "when some corner gets rubbed off by coming in contact with something else." But just so he might become a "polished shaft in the quiver of the Almighty."[7]

What of Nephi's brothers? We've already mentioned that Nephi emphasizes their "stiffneckedness" as he introduces them into the story (1 Ne. 2:11). The text, though, is more hopeful than this suggests. It's especially hopeful when 1 Nephi comes to its conclusion, as we'll see, but it's already more hopeful than we assume when Laman and Lemuel make their first appearance in the text. Laman enters the story when Lehi bestows his name on a river near their desert camp, encouraging him to be "continually running into the fountain of all righteousness" (verse 9). Lehi similarly gives Lemuel's name to the associated valley, encouraging him to be "firm and steadfast, and immovable in keeping the commandments of the Lord" (verse 10). At this point in the text, Nephi has said nothing negative about his brothers. Readers therefore begin with the impression that Lehi feels deeply for his oldest sons, wishing to honor them. But even when Nephi goes on to speak of their unbelief, Laman and Lemuel remain the unique focus of their father's pastoral concern. Lehi names nothing for his younger sons. He upbraids and encourages only Laman and Lemuel in the text. And Nephi reports that Lehi "did speak unto them . . . with power, being filled with the Spirit, until their frames did shake before him" (verse 14).

What we have in this opening sketch is a portrait of resistance and resentment but also of possibility. Laman and Lemuel have their father's focused attention, and they're brought spiritually to their knees by his generous—and overpowering—concern. Laman and Lemuel's introduction doesn't seem meant to poison readers against them. Rather, it seems intended to raise questions about their fate. What will become of these resistant but repentant young men?

Of course, there follow stories in which Laman and Lemuel become violent, threatening harm to Nephi. When things look grim during the Laban encounter, Laman and Lemuel beat "their younger brothers" (1 Ne. 3:28). During their second return to Jerusalem, they bind Nephi "with cords," leaving him "to be devoured by wild beasts" (7:16). They talk openly about killing him after Ishmael's death, hoping "to return again to Jerusalem" (16:36). During a confrontation about building a ship, they attempt to throw Nephi "into the depths of the sea" (17:48). And of course, crossing the ocean, they tie him up "with cords" again, asserting dominance (18:11). Nephi anticipates all these troubles when he initially compares his brothers to those "who sought to take away the life" of Lehi (2:13).

These are uncomfortable stories, despite Nephi's repeated deliverance. They leave us with little sympathy for Laman and Lemuel. But it's unclear if they're meant to be seen as one-sidedly murderous. We've already noted one scholar's argument that Laman and Lemuel are "rather halfhearted assassins." He adds, "Rather than actually stoning or stabbing [Nephi], they threaten him (1 Ne. 16:37; 2 Ne. 5:1–4) or they tie him up (1 Ne. 7:16; 18:11)—actions that could be interpreted as attempts to quiet him or teach him a lesson."[8] In fact, Nephi never once openly criticizes his brothers for their violence toward him—only toward their father (see 1 Ne. 17:44). Indeed, his most consistent criticism, as we've seen, concerns their refusal to trust that God responds and reveals. When they're aggressive toward Nephi, he "frankly forgive[s] them" after they repent (7:21), which they do consistently.

It's particularly interesting that the climactic scene of conflict in 1 Nephi is the most extreme in terms of violence but the least extreme in terms of lasting danger. During the ocean crossing, Nephi reports that his brothers bound him once more, and he adds, "They did treat me with much harshness" (18:11). For once, no one in the company has the power to intervene. When Lehi intercedes, Nephi says his brothers "did breathe out much threatenings against anyone that should speak for [him]" (verse 17). Nephi mentions his "wife with her tears and prayers," as well as his "children," but they unsuccessfully plead for his release (verse 19). This climax in the story of fraternal conflict reaches fever pitch, but Nephi never suggests that his brothers aimed to kill him on the ship. The final quarrel is all show—one that leaves Nephi swollen and sore (see verse 15) but never puts him in mortal danger.

If we're accustomed to seeing these stories in the worst light, it's likely because we look beyond them, anticipating the last conflict story Nephi tells. We learn in 2 Nephi 5 of a final and unresolved attempt on the part of Laman and Lemuel "to take away [Nephi's] life" (5:4). If we know this is coming, we read everything in 1 Nephi as building to that final unresolved conflict. But that story isn't where 1 Nephi ends. It lies beyond 1 Nephi, some chapters into 2 Nephi. Thus the story of Nephi's conflicts with his brothers in *First* Nephi doesn't come to fruition with the final division between two continually warring tribes. That division is the starting point for *Second* Nephi, where it provides context for the prophecies of 2 Nephi 6–30. First Nephi moves through its stories of conflict to a rather different ending.

First Nephi, in fact, concludes on a note of hope for Laman and Lemuel, echoing the way it begins. (This may help to explain the puzzle of the division of Nephi's record into two books.) After so much conflict, the story ends in the promised land, where Nephi's brothers seek the meaning of revelation. The final scene in the book is thus one where Laman and Lemuel ask about Isaiah's prophecies, which Nephi says they should

94

"liken" to their own descendants (1 Ne. 19:24). If we had only 1 Nephi, we'd more naturally see the art in this. Nephi concludes with a scene much like one he saw in vision: Lamanites with "the records of the prophets" in their laps, seeking the "plain and precious" (13:39–40). First Nephi's final lines, in fact, seem directed to all Lamanite readers of the book, not just to Laman and Lemuel: "Wherefore, if ye shall be obedient to the commandments, and endure to the end, ye shall be saved at the last day" (22:31). It's *this* that the whole book yearns for, the full realization of Nephi's "reign and ministry" and a first fulfillment of Lehi's dream. Laman and Lemuel are eating from the fruit of the tree at 1 Nephi's conclusion. Their latter-day descendants are perhaps imagined as doing the same.

Laman and Lemuel have a hard time in 1 Nephi, to be sure. But the book tells the story of their inclusion among those God leads to a New World. And at the book's end, Laman and Lemuel listen as Nephi reads and explains the plainest and most precious prophecies he knows. Second Nephi complicates things, that's its own book. In his first book, Nephi is paternalistic toward his brothers, but he's neither dismissive nor mean to them. It's possible even to suggest that Laman and Lemuel are the book's real heroes, the figures of hope when the curtains come down. Certainly, we have to be more hesitant to draw our natural critical conclusions. Nephi is honest about having helped to create problems that would persist long after his death. He, in fact, tells us that his recognition of difficulties to come was overwhelming, "great above all" (1 Ne. 15:5). But he admirably involves himself in the prophetic effort to provide a solution to the problems he sees with real clarity.

First Nephi has probably done more than anything else to convince us as Latter-day Saints that prophets are perfect. We find in Nephi's story reasons to think that prophets are born better than the rest of us, that they have an easier time being obedient. Nephi's stark sobriety perhaps gives the impression that prophets are humorless or even wooden. We imagine them as grave hermits rather than laughing wise men. It's certainly true that Nephi doesn't force illustrations of his fallibility on his readers. He's far more human than we tend to notice, though. He's honest about his youthful ambition and his fiery temper. He's willing to tell us about how his zeal sometimes outstripped his knowledge and widened the tragic gap between him and his struggling brothers. Now, one might feel that pointing such things out amounts to criticizing the prophet, rejecting his inspiration by showing him to be merely human. And it's true that we *can* have perverse motives in trying to see Nephi's complexity. But the opposite can crucially be true too. To see Nephi's foibles—the foibles he himself shows us—might be to see how much more real the prophetic gift is than our caricatures suggest. The point then wouldn't be to defend our disobedience because the prophets make mistakes. The point would rather be to make clear that we follow the prophets precisely because of what *God* does through them, not because of what or who they are *on their own*.

Nephi is human—wonderfully human. If we read his story with an eye to his humanity, we can find our own experiences reflected in the text. We aren't, you and I, lesser beings struggling to follow the counsel of those who "cannot be touched with the feeling of our infirmities" (Heb. 4:15). Nephi's story is as heartbreaking as our own, but just so it bears within it all the promise that our stories bear. God can do good in and through every fallen human being. If God molded Nephi into a seer, we should have every confidence that he can do the same with us if we're willing to let him. Nephi, in fact, promises us exactly this. The power by which Lehi and Nephi saw visions is "the gift of God unto all those who diligently seek him, as well in times of old . . . as in times to come" (1 Ne. 10:17–19). If we use Nephi's humanity to reject the prophets, we seek only to justify our sins. But if we use Nephi's humanity to see what God might do with us, redemption draws near.

6

The Women

From the very first verse of the Book of Mormon, it feels like women disappear behind men. Nephi says that he was "born of goodly parents," but then he immediately goes on to speak of "the learning" just of his "father" (1 Ne. 1:1). And then Sariah's only major scene in 1 Nephi is when she "complained" about Lehi's being "a visionary man" (5:2). Can't Nephi say something more substantial about the women in his family? Why do women always get the short end of the stick in the Book of Mormon? . . .

a troubled text

Readers find few women in the Book of Mormon, and fewer with names. When women do appear, they're generally nameless and faceless, grouped with the children in the background while men stand at center stage. An alarming number of the stories involving women feature violence, whether attempted or actually accomplished. Consequently, the Book of Mormon feels less and less readable in the twenty-first century, that is, in a culture of progressive emancipation for women. Despite the book's inclusion of some stories of promise for its female characters (for example, Abish), some lament that they have to suppress or ignore an implicit message regarding gender to find value in scripture. And there's reason to think the problem begins in 1 Nephi.[1]

Nephi's brother Jacob claims that God anticipated this whole problem, so visible in the twenty-first century. Jacob cites a series of "commandments" originally "given to our father, Lehi" (Jacob 2:34)—commandments meant to distinguish the New-World Israelite colony from its Old-World counterpart. As the Bible shows, Judah's kings in Jerusalem led the way in reducing women to objects of sexual possession and economic status. According to Lehi, God had heard enough of "the sorrow" and "the mourning of the daughters of [his] people in the land of Jerusalem . . . because of the wickedness and abominations of their husbands" (verse 31). To fix this prevalent Israelite problem, God sent Lehi and his family into the wilderness. "Wherefore, thus saith the Lord," Jacob quotes Lehi saying, "I have led this people forth out of the land of Jerusalem, by the power of mine arm, that I might raise up unto me a righteous branch from the fruit of the loins of Joseph" (verse 25). Israel created an oppressive society for women, but God intended to create new possibilities for Israelite women in a new land.

But cultural change is difficult. According to Jacob, Lehi commanded all his sons, "There shall not any man among you have save it be one wife; and concubines he shall have none" (verse 27). Apparently he added a warning, expecting that men would oppress women in this new colony: "I will not suffer, saith the Lord of Hosts, that the cries of the fair daughters of this people, which I have led out of the land of Jerusalem, shall come up unto me against the men of my people" (verse 32). What would come to the oppressors? Jacob offers his own (rather than Lehi's) word on this point. If Nephite men don't repent of their patterns of sexual oppression, Jacob tells them, the Lamanites "shall scourge [them] even unto destruction" and then "possess the land of [their] inheritance" (3:3–4).

God's worries about Lehi's children were well-founded. It apparently took only a generation for old patterns to reappear among the Nephites, and the rest of the Book of Mormon attests that these patterns continued through Nephite history. Nearly every story about women among the Nephites concerns oppression: commodification, sexual objectification, reduction to prostitution, kidnapping, forced marriage, risky manipulation, violent martyrdom, brutal assault, apocalyptic disaster, torture, rape, and murder. The Nephites fell right into the predicted patterns. It seems significant, moreover, that no women with names in the Book of Mormon are Nephites. They're either biblical (Eve, Sarah, and Mary), pre-Nephite (Sariah), or Lamanite (Abish and Isabel).[2] By contrast, however, it seems the Lamanites kept Lehi's commandments. "They have not forgotten the commandment of the Lord, which was given unto our father," Jacob says to his own people (Jacob 3:5). Through the remainder of the Book of Mormon, Lamanite society avoids the sexual problems of the Nephites.

What evidence is there that something about gender relations was pointed in the right direction among the Lamanites? First, there's a far greater sense of human decency among the Lamanites that affects questions of sexual relationship—such as the simple fact that, unlike Nephite men, Lamanite men don't take advantage of vulnerable women (as in Mosiah 19:13–14). Such stories might well reflect something deeper than just human decency, though. Jacob seems to insinuate as much when he describes the affection that's characteristic of Lamanite families (by explicit contrast with Nephite families). Mutual affection doesn't imply equality, of course, but perhaps Jacob's use of reciprocal formulas does ("their husbands love their wives, and their wives love their husbands"; Jacob 3:7).[3] It's little to go on, and it isn't clear what all it implies, but this sort of talk at least suggests a hint of a promise of equality among the Lamanites. Although the fulfillment of such a promise almost certainly lay a long way off even for the Lamanites, the contrast between apparently benign patriarchy among the Lamanites and devastating violence and oppression for women among the Nephites is noteworthy. We might speak of *relative* equality among the Lamanites—relative to Nephite misogyny. And this is perhaps confirmed by other details, such as the simple fact that our few glimpses into Lamanite society in the Book of Mormon indicate that women wielded political power in Lamanite society that they never did among the Nephites. Especially important here is that queens rule (at least temporarily) when kings are deposed (as in Alma 19:2–11; 47:32–35). By contrast, we have literally no evidence of Nephite women wielding any political power. We don't have a lot of Lamanite cultural data, but what we have suggests that the contrast between their gender culture and that of the Nephites is of prophetic importance.

Despite some promise for women among the Lamanites, because of the appalling Nephite situation it seems God's worries were the right ones, and Jacob's predictions come spectacularly, terribly true. Nephite men, unrepentant of their sins against women, grow worse as the Book of Mormon nears its conclusion. The book ends with Nephite men raping, torturing to death, and finally cannibalizing Lamanite girls—"and they do it for a token of bravery" (Moro. 9:10). The Nephites are accordingly soon eliminated. The Lamanites, however, who maintain relative gender parity throughout their recorded history, experience mercy at the volume's end, despite their other failings. This too Jacob predicts at the outset of Lehite history. Specifically because the Lamanites "observe to keep" Lehi's commandments regarding Israelite gender culture, "the Lord God will not destroy them, but will be merciful unto them; and one day they shall become a blessed people" (Jacob 3:6).

It seems readers are meant to understand that Nephite destruction and Lamanite deliverance both confirm Lehi's and Jacob's warnings about sexual oppression.

The Book of Mormon undeniably presents a depressing picture of the situation for Nephite women. But it also presents some limited prophetic awareness of this situation. It shows a misogynistic society and history, but some of its prophets—lamentably few, but some prophets nonetheless—also warn readers that the problem exists because something went terribly wrong early in Nephite history. But now, how does 1 Nephi contribute to either the historical problem or the prophetic solution? Jacob gave his sermon about Lehi's revelations and Nephite oppression only after Nephi's death. Is it significant, though, that Nephi never mentions Lehi's teachings about gender relations, which he certainly knew (since Lehi died long before he did)? How do women fare in Nephi's writings? The fact is that stories in 1 Nephi involve women more consistently than those in any other book in the Book of Mormon. Does that mean that Nephi sees and helps to identify the problem, or does he write about women in a way that contributes to the problem? How does 1 Nephi compare to the remainder of the Book of Mormon? The question is essential. Readers first encounter the gender culture of the Book of Mormon when they read Nephi's writings, and 1 Nephi all takes place before there's a split between Nephites and Lamanites, before there's a difference between their respective cultures surrounding gender. So how do women fare in 1 Nephi?

We might begin with a few preliminary data points. Only Sariah among the women in 1 Nephi has a name. Ishmael's wife is nameless, as are all of Ishmael's daughters. Since Nephi marries one of Ishmael's daughters (see 1 Ne. 16:7), and since he tells one substantial story about this particular woman (see 18:19), it's remarkable that none of Ishmael's daughters has a name in 1 Nephi. This already tells us something about 1 Nephi's gender culture. It apparently would never occur to Nephi to set women at the heart of the narrative. Further, it seems the woman who bears the male ancestors of all the Lehite tribes receives stronger individual emphasis in 1 Nephi than the women who bear children for those male ancestors. Another point worth mentioning right away is that there's no clear reference to Nephi's sisters anywhere in 1 Nephi (who appear for the first time in 2 Nephi 5:6). With a shock, the reader learns only after finishing 1 Nephi and beginning its sequel that 1 Nephi is populated with not only nameless but also unreferred-to women.[4] It thus seems that Ishmael's daughters stand closer to the center of 1 Nephi than certain other women, despite their own secondary role to Sariah.

All these preliminary data together suggest that there's a kind of hierarchy among women in Nephi's narrative. It's a story first and foremost about Sariah and the daughters of Ishmael, considered to be of distinct relative importance. ☛ But what does 1 Nephi's story about these women amount to? What does it imply about the place of women in Lehite society? And what does it suggest about the place of 1 Nephi in the Book of Mormon's complex presentation of gender?

roles and resistance

Let's begin in earnest with the words Nephi uses to refer to his female characters. Most telling, perhaps, are the patterns of reference for the women who marry Lehi's

☛ Of course, we're ignoring other texts in First Nephi that have implications for its conception of gender: the vision in which Nephi sees the virgin mother of the Lamb and imagines the great and abominable church as the whore of all the earth, and the first quotation of Isaiah that makes Jerusalem a daughter preparing for marriage and uses metaphors of nursing mothers and nursing queens.

sons. When they enter the story, they're "the daughters of Ishmael" (1 Ne. 7:6, 19), but after they're "taken to wife" (16:7), they briefly become "our wives" (verse 27) until Ishmael dies. At that fraught moment in the narrative, these women again and tellingly become "the daughters of Ishmael" rather than the "wives" of Lehi's sons (verse 35). Curiously, though, when conflict over Ishmael's death subsides, Ishmael's daughters don't return to being "our wives" but are instead referred to several times as "our women" (17:1–2, 20). This seems strange, but then one notes that all uses of "our women" in 1 Nephi appear in contexts of childbirth. Once talk of bearing children passes, these women again become "our wives," "their wives," or "my wife" for the remainder of 1 Nephi (18:6, 9, 19).

What's striking about this lexicon, so to speak, is that, despite some variety in how Nephi refers to these women, they're always tied to their social roles. They're the daughters of Ishmael and the wives of Lehi's sons, and they're "women" only when they're giving birth (when they're mothers). These women are literally never individuals. They lack names; they're consistently *of* someone. Since we have Sariah's name in the text, might we guess that she's treated differently? It's true that Sariah has a name in the text, but she's just as consistently tied to a social role as her daughters-in-law. She's never just "Sariah." When her name appears in the text, she's "his wife Sariah" (in 1 Nephi's superscription), "my mother, Sariah" (1 Ne. 2:5; 5:1, 6), or "your mother Sariah" (8:14). And when her name doesn't appear, she's "my mother" (5:3, 7) or "their mother" (18:19). Moreover, Sariah is never called a "woman" in the text (unless she's implicitly among those bearing children in 1 Nephi 17). Thus, although she has a name in 1 Nephi, Sariah is as much absorbed into her social roles as Ishmael's nameless daughters.

It's significant that the women in 1 Nephi are defined by their roles as mothers, wives, daughters, and even "women." This has implications especially for the two moments in the book when women become figures of resistance. It's because Sariah is a mother that she raises questions about her sons' safety, just as it's because the daughters of Ishmael are daughters that they mourn the loss of their father. The social roles these women occupy position them to see things that go unseen by men. It's in fact interesting that all of these women make the actions of Lehi the specific object of their criticisms; the visionary can't see what they can see. At the same time, it's possible to suggest not only that moments of female resistance in 1 Nephi are possible because of the social roles the women occupy but also that moments of female resistance mark a kind of resentment about those social roles—the powerlessness that 1 Nephi's women often experience. Be all that as it may, it's clearly worth asking how 1 Nephi imagines female resistance. How do the two key stories give particular shape to Nephi's portrayal of women?

The two stories of female resistance seem deliberately similar, instances of a single "type scene."[5] Both begin with mourning—Sariah mourning for her sons' presumed death (see 1 Ne. 5:1) and Ishmael's daughters' mourning for their father's real death (see 16:35). In each case, mourning leads to complaint or murmuring and then to confrontation with Lehi. Both stories focus the women's complaint on being led unwillingly from Jerusalem (see 5:2; 16:35). Sariah and Ishmael's daughters alike focus their speech on the family member they've lost: "My sons are no more" (5:2); "our father is dead" (16:35). Both complaints, moreover, culminate in almost the same words of despair about perishing in the wilderness (see 5:2; 16:35). Finally, each story concludes with an expression of confidence in God that's modeled on Nephi's famed statement of zeal in 1 Nephi 3:7. Sariah speaks of knowing that God has given her sons "power whereby they could accomplish the thing which the Lord hath commanded them" (5:8). And the story of Ishmael's daughters concludes with a statement about how God watches out for the faithful, because he "doth nourish them, and strengthen them, and provide means whereby they can accomplish the thing which he has commanded them" (17:3).

These two stories are to be read together. They're linked in ways readers are supposed to recognize. The similarities invite readers to compare the stories, which is aesthetically pleasing. But then the differences between the two stories serve to teach readers something. Similarities draw attention to differences, and differences get at the root of the text's real meaning. It's thus of interest that the two stories at issue in 1 Nephi find their place near the center of each of the book's two halves. The story of Sariah's complaint sits at the center of 1 Nephi 1–9, the abridgment of Lehi's record. And the story of Ishmael's daughters sits at the center of 1 Nephi 10–22, the account of Nephi's own reign and ministry. This suggests that differences between the two stories of female resistance should illustrate the changing situation for women as the first Lehite generation (that of Sariah and Lehi) gives way to the second (that of Sariah's sons and Ishmael's daughters). The first story concerns Sariah, the primordial mother of all Lehite peoples, the woman who dies before the Lehites divide into warring factions. The second story concerns Ishmael's daughters, those women who try to carry on when rivalry between Nephi and Laman becomes dangerous. The first story thus should show how gender relations look before there's a Nephite-Lamanite divide, when Lehi and his concerns about oppression rule the day. The second story should show how gender relations look as the problems of Nephite-Lamanite conflict and history begin.

What's needed, then, is a study of the two stories set side by side. What happens in Sariah's situation of conflict with Lehi? And what happens in turn and by way of contrast when Ishmael's daughters similarly find themselves in conflict with Lehi?

different possibilities for women

Nephi builds the story of Sariah's complaint on a subtle interplay of pronouns. Sariah speaks first in Nephi's recounting: "Behold *thou* hast led *us* forth from the land of *our* inheritance, and *my* sons are no more, and *we* perish in the wilderness" (1 Ne. 5:2; italics added). The variety of pronouns seems important here. With "thou," Sariah separates Lehi from herself, but she immediately follows with "us," perhaps to show that Lehi's actions have implications beyond his own individual situation. This subtly provokes. She then continues with "our inheritance," a phrase that potentially goads as well, since Sariah wouldn't have shared in Lehi's inheritance under then-prevailing laws. Does she mean to claim as shared what her husband likely regarded as his and his sons' alone? ☞ But then Sariah shifts from the plural "our" (referring to land) to the singular "my" when referring to her sons. Sariah seems to claim a share in Lehi's patriarchal inheritance but then grammatically excludes her husband from any proper relationship to their children. Finally, though, Sariah concludes her accusation with the plural "we," which may suggest a

☞ It's possible, of course, that Sariah means to point only to the land the family has lived on, but it seems significant that *our* qualifies *inheritance* rather than *land* (she says "the land of *our* inheritance," not "*our* land of inheritance"). Note also that Nephi reports Laman and Lemuel as regarding this same land as "the land of *their* inheritance" (1 Ne. 2:11; italics added).

109

last glimmer of hope for reconciliation (although, less hopefully, it might refer just to Sariah and her sons).

The variety of the pronouns Sariah uses is striking when set side by side with the unwavering use of pronouns in Lehi's response (see 1 Ne. 5:4–5). He opens his rejoinder with eight consecutive first-person singular pronouns ("I," "my"). Only as he closes does he shift to the more inclusive "us," his own potential gesture of hope for reconciliation (verse 5). The text suggests that Lehi's words don't persuade Sariah. Nephi initially suggests efficacy: "After this manner of language did my father, Lehi, comfort my mother, Sariah" (verse 6). But then Nephi reports, "And when we had returned to the tent of my father, behold their joy was full, and my mother was comforted" (verse 7). This carefully worded report retroactively indicates that Lehi meant to comfort but failed to do so. Only when Sariah saw her sons alive again was she comforted (in a passive construction that leaves Lehi temporarily out of the story). Nephi tells this whole story in a way that superficially suggests conflict between a whining wife and a humble husband but that more subtly suggests an encounter between a rhetorically creative woman and a rhetorically ineffective man.

Importantly, Sariah reconciles with Lehi in the end, and she briefly takes center stage to offer a final beautiful soliloquy. "Now I know of a surety," she says, "that the Lord hath commanded my husband to flee into the wilderness; yea, and I also know of a surety that the Lord hath protected my sons, and delivered them out of the hands of Laban, and given them power whereby they could accomplish the thing which the Lord hath commanded them" (verse 8). This crucially marks the first time Sariah uses the first-person pronoun "I." She uses it to assert her newfound knowledge, clarifying her relationship to the man she now calls "my husband" (in place of her earlier "my sons"). This suggests reconciliation, and on more egalitarian terms than we might expect (although on less egalitarian terms than we might like, to be sure). Sariah is an "I," just as Lehi is. And she attributes all agency to "the Lord" in her exclamation, rather than to her husband. It's thus appropriate that the next verse uses the word "they" to report what happens next. Nephi grammatically unifies his parents when, reconciled, they offer sacrifices together. This may be Nephi's way of ushering Sariah off the stage, but it might also suggest the possibility of a real relationship between his parents.

Such is the trajectory of the episode of Sariah's complaint. She speaks up about her husband's patriarchal control over her family's fate. A rhetorical battle follows, and Sariah appears the abler contender in it. And when circumstances confirm Lehi's calling, Sariah finds deeper trust in God and sees how her husband is under God's influence. The couple reconciles. It's a story of real struggle, and it makes for real catharsis. Now, how does this compare to the parallel story of Ishmael's daughters? Despite deliberate similarities, the two stories end in strikingly different places. The differences prove instructive.

The first signal difference between the two stories is that no one attempts to comfort Ishmael's daughters in their mourning. Where Lehi responds (perhaps indelicately) to Sariah's concerns, no man speaks at all to the mourning women after Ishmael's death. Instead, egregiously, the men within the group speak to other men, and only about still other men: "And Laman said unto Lemuel and also unto the sons of Ishmael: Behold, let us slay our father, and also our brother Nephi, who has taken it upon him to be our ruler and our teacher, who are his elder brethren" (1 Ne. 16:37). Parallels with Sariah's story lead readers to expect here a conflict

between men and women—the complaint provok-
ing an exchange that begins to work toward reconciliation. What we find instead is only a confrontation
between men and men. There's conflict, as anticipated,
but angry young males in the story usurp it, appro-
priating for themselves the women's resistance. And
especially disappointing is the fact that this silences
the women. Ishmael's daughters never speak again in
the story that's meant to be theirs. We feel this especially when the group survives to reach the sea and
everyone is "exceedingly rejoiced" (17:6). The survival
of Sariah's sons provided her an occasion to offer a
monologue that beautifully concludes her fight for her
sex. The whole group's survival might have impressed
the once-mourning daughters of Ishmael, but the
usurpation of their murmuring leaves them unable
to offer a Sariah-like soliloquy at the end of their story.
They remain silent even when they experience divine
deliverance.

Laman usurps the women's complaints, creating a
situation of male-male conflict where the women had
originally initiated one of female-male conflict. But it's
Nephi who usurps what might have been the women's
final expression of newfound trust in God. He concludes the second story of female resistance with words
of his own that echo Sariah's earlier soliloquy: "And if
it so be that the children of men keep the commandments of God he doth nourish them, and strengthen
them, and provide means whereby they can accomplish the thing which he has commanded them" (17:3).
As if to ensure that readers recognize that this replaces
the possible confession of Ishmael's daughters, Nephi
introduces his soliloquy with a note about the women
becoming silent. "And so great were the blessings of
the Lord upon us," Nephi reports, "that while we did

live upon raw meat in the wilderness, our women did give plenty of suck for their children, and were strong, yea, even like unto the men; and they began to bear their journeyings without murmurings" (verse 2). In the place of egalitarian reconciliation between women and men, confirmed by the joyful words of a relieved woman, readers find Nephi's male voice explaining how the women became "like unto the men." This is a different sort of reconciliation, to say the least.

The story of Ishmael's daughters thus lacks the reconciliation that concludes Sariah's story. Female-male conflict, pursued to its conclusion, provokes deeper faith and genuinely shared commitment to God's commandments. But when men usurp female-male conflict and transform it into male-male conflict, there's no expression of deeper faith for the women in the company, just as there's no hint at sharing real commitment to God. There will be further talk of the women's suffering but only as it's weaponized by men in conflict with other men (see verse 20).

First Nephi's two halves thus together tell an unfortunate story about the changing fortunes of women early in New-World Israel's history. In the first generation, that of Sariah and Lehi, conflict between the sexes could play itself out to a productive conclusion. But already with the second generation, that of Nephi and Laman, rivalry between Israelite men became sharp enough that they would appropriate conflict between the sexes, putting women's suffering to work in their own fights for dominance and inheritance. Already in the second half of 1 Nephi, then, we watch as women begin to fall silent. There's a promise of sexual egalitarianism still alive when Sariah and Lehi operate side by side, but it fades as the next generation privileges its own nonegalitarian concerns. We can thus track the developments that may well have led Lehi to try to speak of God's hope for women in the new colony. First Nephi simultaneously envisions a place for women willing to resist oppression *and* recounts the circumstances in which that place of resistance is eliminated.

First Nephi exhibits a tension that then underlies the whole of Nephite history. Nephi marks with the story of Sariah's complaint the possibility of a cultural understanding of gender radically different from what later takes hold. But he also tracks how certain conflicts largely eliminate that possibility right at the beginning of Nephite history. First Nephi thus briefly gives readers cause to rejoice, but then it gives them much greater "cause to mourn" (Hel. 15:2). Things might have been different. They weren't. But precisely for this reason, 1 Nephi—like the whole Book of Mormon—might provide an ironic and deeply affecting occasion to "give thanks unto God." It displays the Nephites' "imperfections" and encourages readers to "be more wise" than they were (Morm. 9:31).

The Nephite prophets are intriguingly paradoxical. They're products in part of oppressive cultures, societies we'd find difficult to live in with our modern sensibilities. And these prophets often retain cultural attitudes that make us cringe today. None of this is surprising. What's remarkable is that, even as they sometimes embody cultural attitudes that concern us, they themselves see and earnestly struggle against those attitudes. Nephi makes derogatory comments about the emerging Lamanite people (see 2 Ne. 5:19–25), but he also provides the Book of Mormon's clearest testimony that God draws no racial distinctions (see 26:33). Similarly, the near-invisibility of women in Nephi's record leaves us with questions regarding his assumptions about gender, and yet it's Nephi who tells us the stories that reveal how the situation for women took a terrible turn early in Nephite history. In the end, I suspect that the definition of a prophet includes embodying paradox. The prophets are enmeshed in human affairs, as much a part of the human predicament as anyone else, but they're somehow able to *see* the problems to which we all contribute. They represent a site of dynamic struggle from within and yet against unrighteousness, not a static position of exception outside of it.

For this reason, we succeed only in being hypocrites if we quickly pass judgment on Nephi for what seems to us his moral failings. First Nephi should teach us that our struggles against unrighteousness aren't new. We're as enmeshed in oppressive cultures as the prophets of the past, and we're almost certainly blind to our own prejudices. We live in a time of gradual emancipation for women, but our society has proven itself as likely as ancient Israel to reduce women to certain social roles, to make them into objects of possession and oppression, and to allow male interests to usurp women's struggles for recognition. Nephi's record might provide us with a clearer sense of what it means to get the relations between the sexes right in modern Israel by showing us how things went wrong—and how they're still going wrong among ourselves too often. Then we'd have reason indeed to thank God for this remarkable record.

Conclusion

The Latter-day Saint scholar I hold in highest esteem is—and I think always will be—Hugh Nibley. It was in reading Nibley's writings that I first experienced what the life of the mind could be. And it was crucial for me that Nibley was as skeptical about as he was entranced by scholarship. He arguably gave more time and attention to academic work than anyone else has (or soon will) in the Restoration. But he coupled this intellectual obsession with a striking cynicism about what the intellect can do. He had no illusions about the secular academy being an unbiased assembly of truth-seekers. But he nonetheless gave everything he had to the task of seeking truth. In my view, Nibley struck the balance between faith and reason perfectly. And it was in the light that Nibley used to shine on things that I first really saw Nephi. Reading Nibley's *Lehi in the Desert*, I discovered the Nephi of history. Nibley showed me a Nephi who really did wake up one morning in Jerusalem to find that his father was packing to leave the city. He showed me a Nephi whose writings fit comfortably in the realities of Arabian desert life. Nibley showed me a Nephi who lived and breathed in a very real ancient world.

I'm not a historian. I can't add much that's of a historical nature to Nibley's remarkable portrait of Nephi. I did once dream of doing the kind of work Nibley did, but God pressed me toward another field of research. I'm a theologian who specializes in the close reading of texts. Because I lack the training, then, I have to leave to others the furthering of Nibley's historical work. But I have something of my own to contribute. I hope the preceding chapters add something of immense importance to our picture of Nephi, something difficult for historians to discern as they do their own invaluable work. At any rate, when I work my way through 1 Nephi, I find a carefully ordered theological project. It has specific and discernible purposes and a deeply prophetic message. It offers itself as the product of an inspired mind, the careful work of a seer who gave his life to writing as plainly as possible about the extraordinary visions granted him by God. I find also in 1 Nephi an autobiographical sketch that reveals the humanity as well as the divinity of this remarkable prophet. Nephi is an honest prophet, a chosen vessel but still an earthen vessel. And so I find in 1 Nephi a subtle but crucial prophetic humility that's inspiring in its own way.

Disarmingly human but extraordinarily gifted with prophecy—this is the Nephi I'd follow into the desert. In fact, it's the Nephi I *have* followed into the desert. I've traveled with Nephi, as it were, to where he stood when the Spirit swept him away to witness the history of his people. I've sat by the seaside with him as he's told me about his struggles with his brothers. I've followed him into the wilderness of Isaiah's writings and learned as he's taught me to read them. The Nephi who lived through some experiences I'm grateful never to have had and whose other experiences I hope I can and will have some day—the Nephi who then took decades to reflect on these experiences and several years more to give them a shape that could speak to me—*I love this Nephi*. He's taught me more than any other source the meaning of the Restoration. He was the first to show me my real place in history. What an angelic guide once was to Nephi, Nephi has himself been to me. I don't know the meaning of all things, but Nephi has made me feel God's love for his children in ways I couldn't have experienced without him.

The very first story in 1 Nephi concerns a time when a divine being descended from heaven to bring a book to Lehi. When Lehi read that heavenly book, Nephi tells us, "he was filled with the Spirit of the Lord" (1 Ne. 1:12). This is *my* experience exactly with Nephi's own writings. They've come to me from above, like a heavenly record. They're a grace, over and over a grace. And this heavenly book has filled me with the Spirit of the Lord. I long for goodness in part because I've read Nephi's words. I long for God in part because of how Nephi has taught me to see him. And so I thank God for Nephi.

Further Reading

Little of a strictly theological nature has been written on 1 Nephi. The essays in Adam S. Miller, ed., *A Dream, a Rock, and a Pillar of Fire: Reading 1 Nephi 1* (Provo, UT: Neal A. Maxwell Institute, 2017), may constitute the only collection of sustained theological reflections specifically on this book (and these are limited to reflections on 1 Nephi 1). A gathering of more traditional "doctrinal" studies of 1 Nephi is Monte S. Nyman and Charles D. Tate, eds., *The Book of Mormon: First Nephi, The Doctrinal Foundation* (Provo, UT: BYU Religious Studies Center, 1989).

Most of the scholarly work that has been done on 1 Nephi is historical in nature, usually aimed at defending the antiquity of the Book of Mormon. For a representative collection of essays, see John W. Welch, David Rolph Seely, and Jo Ann H. Seely, eds., *Glimpses of Lehi's Jerusalem* (Provo, UT: FARMS, 2004). The most important historical treatment of 1 Nephi remains Hugh Nibley, *Lehi in the Desert/ The World of the Jaredites/ There Were Jaredites*, ed. John W. Welch (Salt Lake City and Provo, UT: Deseret Book and FARMS, 1988), 1–149. Other important essays appear in S. Kent Brown, *From Jerusalem to Zarahemla: Literary and Historical Studies of the Book of Mormon* (Provo, UT: BYU Religious Studies Center, 1998).

The best treatment of Nephi as a literary artist is Grant Hardy, *Understanding the Book of Mormon: A Reader's Guide* (New York: Oxford University Press, 2010), 31–57. Another interesting take is Claudia

L. Bushman, "I, Nephi," in *Perspectives on Mormon Theology: Scriptural Theology*, ed. James E. Faulconer and Joseph M. Spencer (Salt Lake City: Greg Kofford Books, 2015), 81–95. An important alternative proposal regarding the literary structure of 1 Nephi appears in Noel B. Reynolds, "Nephi's Outline," in *Book of Mormon Authorship: New Light on Ancient Origins*, ed. Noel B. Reynolds (Provo, UT: FARMS, 1982), 53–74.

For a good recent survey and critique of the literature on the slaying of Laban, see Charles Swift, "'The Lord Slayeth the Wicked': Coming to Terms with Nephi Killing Laban," *Journal of Book of Mormon Studies* 28 (2019): 137–69. Of course, by far the best-known treatment is John W. Welch, "Legal Perspectives on the Slaying of Laban," *Journal of Book of Mormon Studies* 1, no. 1 (1992): 119–41.

Much has been written on Lehi's dream, and from a variety of perspectives. Two particularly interesting collections of essays are Daniel L. Belnap, Gaye Strathearn, and Stanley A. Johnson, eds., *The Things Which My Father Saw: Approaches to Lehi's Dream and Nephi's Vision* (Salt Lake City and Provo, UT: Deseret Book and BYU Religious Studies Center, 2011); and John W. Welch and Donald W. Parry, eds. *The Tree of Life from Eden to Eternity* (Salt Lake City and Provo, UT: Deseret Book and Neal A. Maxwell Institute, 2011). Noteworthy articles include those by Amy Easton-Flake, Grant Hardy, and Daniel Belnap in the former collection and those by Charles Swift and Richard Oman in the latter.

Important studies of Nephi's vision include (in addition to essays from the two just-mentioned collections) Stephen E. Robinson, "Early Christianity and 1 Nephi 13–14," in *First Nephi, The Doctrinal Foundation*, 177–91; and Shon D. Hopkin, "Seeing Eye to Eye: Nephi's and John's Intertwining Visions of the Tree of Life," in

Apocalypse: Reading Revelation 21–22, ed. Julie M. Smith (Provo, UT: Neal A. Maxwell Institute, 2016), 66–84.

The traditional approach to the Isaiah texts that appear in 1 Nephi can be seen in Victor L. Ludlow, *Unlocking Isaiah in the Book of Mormon* (Salt Lake City: Deseret Book, 2003), 34–60. More academic treatments can be found in Brown, *From Jerusalem to Zarahemla*, 9–27; and Andrew C. Skinner, "Nephi's Lessons to His People: The Messiah, the Land, and Isaiah 48–49 in 1 Nephi 19–22," in *Isaiah in the Book of Mormon*, ed. Donald W. Parry and John W. Welch (Provo, UT: FARMS, 1998), 95–122. A far more robust treatment appears in my own study of the subject, Joseph M. Spencer, *The Vision of All: Twenty-Five Lectures on Isaiah in Nephi's Record* (Salt Lake City: Greg Kofford Books, 2016), 1–117.

Unfortunately, there few studies of women specifically in 1 Nephi. An attempt to recover female voices from the historical record appears in Camille Fronk, "Desert Epiphany: Sariah and the Women in 1 Nephi," *Journal of Book of Mormon Studies* 9, no. 2 (2000): 4–15, 80. A few additional insights appear in Jerrie W. Hurd, *Our Sisters in the Latter-Day Scriptures* (Salt Lake City: Deseret Book, 1987), 1–11; and Heather B. Moore, *Women of the Book of Mormon: Insights and Inspirations* (American Fork, UT: Covenant Communications, 2010), 11–19.

Endnotes

SERIES INTRODUCTION

1. Elder Neal A. Maxwell, "The Children of Christ," Devotional Address, Brigham Young University, 4 February 1990, https://speeches.byu.edu/talks/neal-a-maxwell_children-christ/ (accessed 16 April 2019).

2. Elder Neal A. Maxwell, "The Inexhaustible Gospel," Devotional Address, Brigham Young University, 18 August 1992, https://speeches.byu.edu/talks/neal-a-maxwell/inexhaustible-gospel/ (accessed 6 August 2019).

3. Elder Neal A. Maxwell, "The Book of Mormon: A Great Answer to 'The Great Question,'" Book of Mormon Symposium Address, Brigham Young University, 10 October 1986, reprinted in *The Voice of My Servants: Apostolic Messages on Teaching, Learning, and Scripture,* eds. Scott C. Esplin and Richard Neitzel Holzapfel (Provo, UT: Religious Studies Center, Brigham Young University; Salt Lake City: Deseret Book, 2010), 221–38, https://rsc.byu.edu/archived/voice-my-servants/book-mormon-great-answer-great-question (accessed 16 April 2019).

INTRODUCTION

1. Neal A. Maxwell, *Not My Will, but Thine* (Salt Lake City: Bookcraft, 1988), 33.

1

1. For more on comparing the opening of Nephi's record and the book of Genesis, see Grant Hardy, *Understanding the Book of Mormon: A Reader's Guide* (New York: Oxford University Press, 2010), 12–16.

2. The structural analyses in this chapter draw on Joseph M. Spencer, *The Vision of All: Twenty-Five Lectures on Isaiah in Nephi's Record* (Salt Lake City: Greg Kofford Books, 2016), 37–58; and Joseph M. Spencer,

An Other Testament: On Typology, 2nd ed. (Provo, UT: Neal A. Maxwell Institute, 2016), xiv–xvi, 33–104. See also Frederick W. Axelgard, "1 and 2 Nephi: An Inspiring Whole," *BYU Studies* 26, no. 4 (Fall 1986): 53–66.

3. On the original chapter breaks in the Book of Mormon, see Royal Skousen, *Analysis of Textual Variants of the Book of Mormon*, 2nd ed. (Provo, UT: FARMS, 2017), 45–48. Original chapters are easily visible in Grant Hardy, ed., *The Book of Mormon, Another Testament of Jesus Christ: Maxwell Institute Study Edition* (Salt Lake City and Provo, UT: Deseret Book, Neal A. Maxwell Institute, and BYU Religious Studies Center, 2018).

2

1. Interpretations set forth in this chapter repurpose parts of Spencer, *Vision of All*, 2–11; and Spencer, *An Other Testament*, 34–40.

2. Heather Hardy, "The Double Nature of God's Saving Work: The Plan of Salvation and Salvation History," in *The Things Which My Father Saw: Approaches to Lehi's Dream and Nephi's Vision*, ed. Daniel L. Belnap, Gaye Strathearn, and Stanley A. Johnson (Salt Lake City and Provo, UT: Deseret Book and BYU Religious Studies Center, 2011), 15–36.

3. For a helpful introduction to changing attitudes about Israelite salvation history in early Christianity, see Judith M. Lieu, *Christian Identity in the Jewish and Graeco-Roman World* (New York: Oxford University Press, 2004).

4. This is the reading of the earliest text. See Skousen, *Analysis of Textual Variants of the Book of Mormon*, 2nd ed. (Provo, UT: FARMS, 2017), 235–38.

5. For standard readings of Nephi's use of Isaiah 48–49 in 1 Nephi, see S. Kent Brown, *From Jerusalem to Zarahemla: Literary and Historical Studies of the Book of Mormon* (Provo, UT: BYU Religious Studies Center, 1998), 9–27; Andrew C. Skinner, "Nephi's Lessons to His People: The Messiah, the Land, and Isaiah 48–49 in 1 Nephi 19–22," in *Isaiah in the Book of Mormon*, ed. Donald W. Parry and John W. Welch (Provo, UT: FARMS, 1998), 100–4; and Hardy, *Understanding the Book of Mormon*, 70–74.

3

1. See Joseph Fielding McConkie and Robert L. Millet, *Doctrinal Commentary on the Book of Mormon*, 4 vols. (Salt Lake City: Bookcraft, 1987–1992), 1:77–85, 2:226–29.

2. For some helpful information about the ambiguities of the image of "the Lamb of God," see David E. Aune, *Revelation 1–5*, Word Biblical Commentary (Dallas: Thomas Nelson, 1997), 367–73.

3. For some context regarding Lehi's opposition in Jerusalem regarding his teaching about the Messiah, see Joseph M. Spencer, "Potent Messianism: Textual, Historical, and Theological Notes on 1 Nephi 1:18–20," in *A Dream, a Rock, and a Pillar of Fire: Reading 1 Nephi 1*, ed. Adam S. Miller (Provo, UT: Neal A. Maxwell Institute, 2017), 47–74. A good theological unpacking of the peculiar Nephite doctrine of the Messiah appears in Adam S. Miller, *An Early Resurrection: Life in Christ before You Die* (Salt Lake City and Provo, UT: Deseret Book and Neal A. Maxwell Institute, 2018).

4. Scholars debate the details about how this spirit of anticipation developed, how widespread it was at any given time, and how frequently the anticipatory vision included hope—rather than vengeance—for the nations. The general contours are, however, a matter of consensus.

5. For discussion, see Skousen, *Analysis of Textual Variants*, 263–64.

6. See Skousen, *Analysis of Textual Variants*, 235–38.

4

1. The argument in this chapter develops ideas first laid out in Joseph M. Spencer, "René Girard and Mormon Scripture: A Response," *Dialogue: A Journal of Mormon Thought* 43, no. 3 (Fall 2010): 6–20; and Spencer, *An Other Testament*, 84–90.

2. Eugene England, "Why Nephi Killed Laban: Reflections on the Truth of the Book of Mormon," *Dialogue: A Journal of Mormon Thought* 22, no. 3 (Fall 1989): 42. By way of example, England mentions parenthetically that Ron and Dan Lafferty used Nephi's words in court to justify their murder of Brenda and Erica Lafferty in 1984.

3. John W. Welch, "Legal Perspectives on the Slaying of Laban," *Journal of Book of Mormon Studies* 1, no. 1 (1992): 121.

4. Jeffrey R. Holland, "How Can I Explain Nephi's Killing Laban to My Nonmember Friends?" *Ensign*, September 1976, 84.

5. Charles Swift, "'The Lord Slayeth the Wicked': Coming to Terms with Nephi Killing Laban," *Journal of Book of Mormon Studies* 28 (2019): 143.

6. The best representative of the legal approach to the episode is Welch, "Legal Perspectives."

7. England, "Why Nephi Killed Laban," 43.

8. For the classic version of this approach to the Abraham-and-Isaac story, see Søren Kierkegaard, *Fear and Trembling*, trans. Alastair Hannay (New York: Penguin Books, 1986).

9. Important literary treatments include Ben McGuire, "Nephi and Goliath: A Case Study of Literary Allusion in the Book of Mormon," *Journal of the Book of Mormon and Other Restoration Scripture* 18, no. 1 (2009): 16–31; and Steven L. Olsen, "The Death of Laban: A Literary Interpretation," *FARMS Review* 21, no. 1 (2009): 179–95.

10. Swift, "'The Lord Slayeth the Wicked'" 157.

5

1. England, "Why Nephi Killed Laban," 40.

2. Grant Hardy, *Understanding the Book of Mormon: A Reader's Guide* (New York: Oxford University Press, 2010), 39–40.

3. For the political reading of Nephi's record, see Noel B. Reynolds, "The Political Dimension in Nephi's Small Plates," *BYU Studies* 27, no. 4 (1987): 1–24; and Val Larsen, "Killing Laban: The Birth of Sovereignty in the Nephite Constitutional Order," *Journal of Book of Mormon Studies* 16, no. 1 (2007): 26–41.

4. Swift, "'The Lord Slayeth the Wicked,'" 157.

5. S. Kent Brown suggests that the giving of "burnt offerings" (1 Ne. 5:9) after the episode means something is amiss about the whole experience. See Brown, *From Jerusalem to Zarahemla*, 4–6.

6. See Skousen, *Analysis of Textual Variants*, 152–54.

7. Joseph Smith Jr., *History of the Church of Jesus Christ of Latter-day Saints*, ed. B. H. Roberts, 7 vols. (Salt Lake City: Deseret Book, 1971), 5:401.

8. Hardy, *Understanding the Book of Mormon*, 39.

6

1. The approach in this chapter is preliminarily presented in Kimberly Berkey and Joseph M. Spencer, "'Great Cause to Mourn': The Complexity of *The Book of Mormon*'s Presentation of Gender and Race," in *Americanist Approaches to* The Book of Mormon, ed. Elizabeth Fenton and Jared Hickman (New York: Oxford University Press, 2019), 298–320. For a similar reading of Jacob 1–3, worked out in some detail, see Deidre Green's volume on the book of Jacob in the present book series. The most sophisticated survey treatments of women in the Book of Mormon are, at the theoretical level, Camille S. Williams, "Women in the Book of Mormon: Inclusion, Exclusion, and Interpretation," *Journal of Book of Mormon Studies* 11 (2002): 66–79, 111–14; and, at the textual level, Jerrie W. Hurd, *Our Sisters in the Latter-day Scriptures* (Salt Lake City: Deseret Book, 1987). The most important critical treatments remain Carol Lynn Pearson, "Could Feminism Have Saved the Nephites?" *Sunstone* 19, no. 1 (March 1996): 32–40; and Lynn Matthews Anderson, "Toward a Feminist Interpretation of Latter-day Scripture," *Dialogue: A Journal of Mormon Thought* 27, no. 2 (Summer 1994): 185–203.

2. There's some ambiguity about Isabel, who hails from "the land of Siron among the borders of the Lamanites" (Alma 39:3).

3. It's striking that Zeniff speaks of "that which was good" among the Lamanites (Mosiah 9:1). Given Zeniff's patterns of care for women (and others marginalized by the Nephites), this seems to have gendered implications. On Zeniff's character, see Hardy, *Understanding the Book of Mormon*, 123–32.

4. Some speculate that Nephi's sisters are the wives of the already-married sons of Ishmael (see 1 Ne. 7:6), but this isn't clear. See John L. Sorenson, *Nephite Culture and Society: Selected Papers* (Salt Lake City: New Sage Books, 1997), 1–24.

5. Robert Alter defines scriptural type scenes as "recurrent narrative episodes" that are "dependent on the manipulation of a fixed constellation of predetermined motifs." Alter, *The Art of Biblical Narrative* (New York: Basic Books, 1981), 51.

Editions of the
Book of Mormon

Most Latter-day Saints are familiar principally with the official edition of the Book of Mormon published in 2013 by the Church of Jesus Christ of Latter-day Saints. It contains the canonical text of the book, divided into chapters of relatively even length with numbered verses for ease of access. Its footnotes aim to assist readers in seeking doctrinal understanding.

Other Book of Mormon editions are available and often helpful. Among these are official editions from earlier in the scripture's publishing history, which are relatively accessible. There are also editions published recently by a variety of presses meant to make the text more readable. Both types of editions are referred to throughout *Book of Mormon: brief theological introductions*. Also of importance (and occasionally referred to) are the manuscript sources for the printed editions of the Book of Mormon.

manuscript sources

Unfortunately, the original manuscript of the Book of Mormon was damaged during the nineteenth century, but substantial portions of it remain. All known extant portions have been published in typescript in Royal Skousen, ed., *The Original Manuscript of the Book of Mormon: Typographical Facsimile of the Extant Text* (Provo, UT: FARMS, 2001). A future volume of the Joseph Smith Papers will publish images of the extant manuscript, along with a typescript.

After completing the original manuscript's dictation, Joseph Smith assigned Oliver Cowdery to produce a second manuscript copy of the text. That manuscript has been called the printer's manuscript since it was designed for use by the first printer of the Book of Mormon. The printer's manuscript, which is more or less entirely intact, also contains corrections and other editorial markings inserted when the second (1837) edition of the Book of Mormon was being prepared. A typescript of the printer's manuscript can be found in Royal Skousen, ed., *The Printer's Manuscript of the Book of Mormon: Typographical Facsimile of the Entire Text in Two Parts,* 2 vols. (Provo, UT: FARMS, 2001). Full color images of the manuscript were subsequently published along with a transcript in the Joseph Smith Papers series: Royal Skousen and Robin Scott Jensen, eds., *Printer's Manuscript of the Book of Mormon*, 2 vols., vol. 3 of the *Revelations and Translations* series of The Joseph Smith Papers, ed. Dean C. Jessee, Ronald K. Esplin, and Richard Lyman Bushman (Salt Lake City: Church Historian's Press, 2015). The images and transcript of the printer's manuscript are also available at the Joseph Smith Papers website (www.josephsmithpapers.org/the-papers/revelations-and-translations/jsppr3).

historical editions

Multiple editions of the Book of Mormon were published during the lifetime of Joseph Smith. The first edition, published in Palmyra, New York, in 1830, appeared without versification and with fewer chapter divisions than the present canonical text. The text of the 1830 edition is available electronically at the Joseph Smith Papers website (www.josephsmithpapers.org/the-papers/revelations-and-translations/jsppr4) and in print through various publishers as a replica edition. The 1830 text is also available in Robert A. Rees and Eugene England, eds., *The Reader's Book of Mormon* (Salt Lake City: Signature Books, 2008), which is divided into seven pocket-sized volumes (each with an introduction by a scholar).

Joseph Smith introduced numerous minor changes into the text of the Book of Mormon when it was prepared for a second edition in 1837. Many of these changes are marked in the printer's manuscript. Most were aimed at correcting grammatical issues, but some, in a small handful of cases, were also aimed at clarifying the meaning of the text or its doctrinal implications. The 1837 edition is available electronically at the Joseph Smith Papers website (www.josephsmithpapers.org/the-papers/revelations-and-translations/jsppr4).

A third edition was prepared under Joseph Smith's direction in 1840, and evidence makes clear that the original manuscript was consulted carefully in preparing this edition. Some important errors in the earlier editions were corrected, further grammatical improvements were introduced, and a few other changes were made to the text for purposes of clarification. The 1840 edition can be read at the Joseph Smith Papers website (www.josephsmithpapers.org/the-papers/revelations-and-translations/jsppr4). It forms the basis for at least one printed edition as well: *The Book of Mormon*, trans. Joseph Smith Jr. (New York: Penguin Books, 2008), which contains

THE

BOOK OF MORMON:

AN ACCOUNT WRITTEN BY THE HAND OF MOR-
MON, UPON PLATES TAKEN FROM
THE PLATES OF NEPHI.

Wherefore it is an abridgment of the Record of the People of Nephi; and also of
the Lamanites; written to the Lamanites, which are a remnant of the House of
Israel; and also to Jew and Gentile; written by way of commandment, and also
by the spirit of Prophesy and of Revelation. Written, and sealed up, and hid
up unto the LORD, that they might not be destroyed; to come forth by the gift
and power of GOD unto the interpretation thereof; sealed by the hand of Moroni, and hid up unto the LORD, to come forth in due time by the way of Gentile;
the interpretation thereof by the gift of GOD; an abridgment taken from the
Book of Ether.

Also, which is a Record of the People of Jared, which were scattered at the time
the LORD confounded the language of the people when they were building a
tower to get to Heaven; which is to shew unto the remnant of the House of
Israel how great things the LORD hath done for their fathers; and that they may
know the covenants of the LORD, that they are not cast off forever; and also to
the convincing of the Jew and Gentile that JESUS is the CHRIST, the ETERNAL
GOD, manifesting Himself unto all nations. And now if there be fault, it be the
mistake of men; wherefore condemn not the things of GOD, that ye may be
found spotless at the judgment seat of CHRIST.

BY JOSEPH SMITH, JUNIOR,
AUTHOR AND PROPRIETOR.

PALMYRA:

PRINTED BY E. B. GRANDIN, FOR THE AUTHOR.

1830.

FIGURE 11 The title page of the original 1830 edition of The Book of
Mormon. © Intellectual Reserve, Inc.

a helpful introduction by Laurie Maffly-Kipp, a scholar of American religious history.

One other edition of the Book of Mormon appeared during the lifetime of Joseph Smith—an 1841 British edition, which was largely based on the 1837 edition and therefore lacked corrections and other improvements that appear in the 1840 edition. It, too, is available electronically at the Joseph Smith Papers website (www.josephsmithpapers.org/the-papers/revelations-and-translations/jsppr4).

In 1879, Latter-day Saint apostle Orson Pratt completed one of the more influential editions of the Book of Mormon published after Joseph Smith's death. Pratt lamented that too many Latter-day Saints left the scripture unread on the shelf. He sought to create an easier reading experience by dividing up the originally long chapters and adding verse numbers—revisions which have largely remained unchanged in the Church's official edition to the present. He also pioneered a system of cross-references and other explanatory foot-notes. Most of Pratt's notes were removed or replaced in subsequent official editions—most thoroughly in the Church's 1981 edition when new descriptive chapter headings were introduced. These headings can still be found, with a few minor updates, in the 2013 edition.

A detailed and helpful devotional treatment of the publication history of the Book of Mormon can be found in Richard E. Turley Jr. and William W. Slaughter, *How We Got the Book of Mormon* (Salt Lake City: Deseret Book, 2011). These authors trace developments in the format and study apparatuses used to present the text of the Book of Mormon to audiences from the 1850s to the present.

study and reading editions

The most important scholarly editions of the Book of Mormon are Grant Hardy, ed., *The Book of Mormon: A Reader's Edition* (Urbana and Chicago: University of Illinois Press, 2003); and Royal Skousen, ed., *The Book of Mormon: The Earliest Text* (New Haven, CT: Yale University Press, 2009).

Hardy's edition repackages the text of the 1921 public domain edition of the Book of Mormon. It contains a helpful introduction, a series of useful appendices, and a straightforward presentation of the text in a highly readable format. Footnotes are minimal—they are used only to clarify direct references or allusions within the text, to track dates, or to alert readers about original chapter divisions. This edition contains modern chapter and verse divisions, but they are unobtrusively typeset. The text is presented in straightforward paragraphs, with one-line headings marking text divisions. Poetry is set off in poetic lines, as in modern editions of the Bible.

Skousen's edition is the result of his quarter-century-long work with the manuscript and printed sources for the Book of Mormon text. The edition aims to reproduce as closely as can be reconstructed the words originally dictated by Joseph Smith to his scribes. Chapter and verse divisions familiar from recent editions are in the text (and symbols mark original chapter breaks), but the text is presented in what Skousen calls "sense lines"—each line containing (on Skousen's reconstruction) approximately what the prophet would have dictated at one time before pausing to allow his scribe to write. The edition contains helpful introductory material and a summary appendix noting significant differences between *The Earliest Text* and the current official edition. It is otherwise without any apparatus for the reader.

The most significant edition of the Book of Mormon deliberately constructed for a lay reading audience is Grant Hardy, ed., *The Book of Mormon: Another Testament of Jesus Christ, Maxwell Institute Study Edition* (Salt Lake City and Provo, UT: Neal A. Maxwell Institute, Deseret Book, and BYU Religious Studies Center, 2018). In this edition, Hardy uses the text of the 2013 official edition of the Book of Mormon but presents it in a readable way for everyday students of the volume. This edition reproduces the best of what appears in Hardy's *Reader's Edition* but adds further resources in the introductory and appendix materials. The footnotes are updated and expanded to include variant readings from the original and printer's manuscripts, and to provide notes about other textual details. The body of the text is presented, as in the *Reader's Edition*, in a straightforward fashion, readable and interrupted only by one-line headings. Modern chapter and verse divisions, as well as original chapter divisions, are easily visible.

Index

143

Colophon

The text of the book is typeset in Arnhem,
Fred Smeijer's 21st-century-take on late
18th-century Enlightenment-era letterforms
known for their sturdy legibility and clarity
of form. Captions and figures are typset in
Quaadraat Sans, also by Fred Smeijers.
The book title and chapter titles are typeset
in Thema by Nikola Djurek.

Printed on Domtar Lynx 74 gsm,
Forest Stewardship Council (FSC) Certified.

Printed by Brigham Young University Print & Mail Services

Woodcut illuminations **Brian Kershisnik**
Book design & typography **Douglas Thomas**

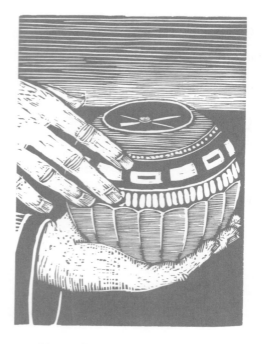

1 Nephi 16:10 he beheld upon the ground a
round ball of curious workmanship